Attendin
Children

Direct Work in Social and Health Care

Margaret Crompton

Edward Arnold
A division of Hodder & Stoughton
LONDON   MELBOURNE   AUCKLAND

© 1990 Margaret Crompton

First published in Great Britain 1990

British Library Cataloguing in Publication Data
Crompton, Margaret *1941–*
  Attending to children: direct work in social and health care.
  1. Great Britain. Welfare work with children
  I. Title
  362.70941

  ISBN 0–340–52741–2

Whilst the advice and information in this book is believed to be true
and accurate at the date of going to press, neither the author nor the
publisher can accept any legal responsibility or liability for any errors
or omissions that may be made. In particular (but without limiting the
generality of the preceding disclaimer) every effort has been made to
check drug dosages; however, it is still possible that errors have been
missed. Furthermore, dosage schedules are being continually revised
and new side-effects recognized. For these reasons the reader is
strongly urged to consult the drug companies' printed instructions
before administering any of the drugs recommended in this book.

Typeset in Times/Univers by Butler & Tanner Ltd, Frome and London
Printed and bound in Great Britain for Edward Arnold,
a division of Hodder and Stoughton Limited,
Mill Road, Dunton Green, Sevenoaks, Kent TN13 2YA
by Biddles Limited, Guildford and King's Lynn

Contents

Introduction   v

PART 1   1

1   How to love a child   3

2   Look up from despair   10

PART 2   25

3   Beginning with ending   27

4   Begin at the beginning   40

PART 3   51

5   From fear to trust   53

6   Speak the truth in love   63

7   I know what you mean   68

8   Be here now   76

PART 4   85

9   Talking without words   87

10 Everyminute communication   102

Conclusion   117

Bibliography   118

Author index   123

Subject index   125

Introduction

Warsaw 1981, *Andrzej* lies on his bed. His parents stand beside him, awkward, shy. The young doctor showing us round the hospital ignores them. I am amazed, hurt. I know he is gentle and courteous. How can he suddenly be so rude? But he is being kind. Visitors are not allowed. If he acknowledges the existence of *Andrzej's* parents he must ask them to leave. If he attends to the parents, they may not attend to their child.

My visit to Poland where, with my husband, I studied aspects of child care and education, took place a few months after publication of my book *Respecting Children* (1980). Experience on which *Attending To Children* is based includes that visit, research into provisions for young people in trouble with the law, writing on adolescents, co-editing a book on education, occasional social work as a guardian *ad litem* and for a social services department family placement unit, and freelance lecturing.

The philosophy from which *Respecting Children* developed has not changed and has, if anything, been confirmed in the 10-year interval. I believe that workers in whatever field and with whatever focus can effectively respect and attend to children only if they respect and attend to themselves and one another. Needs are so great and resources so limited, that there is no margin for any waste of time, money, energy or love.

This book is representative of my own experience and thinking, rather than that of any particular theoretical base. I believe in giving full attention to the whole person, being direct and honest and using the most simple and least intrusive methods and equipment. There is, of course, always a gap between intention and achievement, philosophy and practice, often because of heavy crisis-ridden case loads, poor support and administrative demands. However, firm belief in an ideal is essential if workers are to offer children effective service and care.

Because *Attending To Children* is written for a multi-disciplinary readership, including students and practitioners, reference is made to literature and practice from a number of fields. Use is made also of a variety of fictional sources, including children's books, and of philosophy, sociology and religion, as these are as illuminating as 'professional' texts. Extracts and examples are, necessarily, brief.

With the exception of references from North American and Polish literature, almost all practice examples are drawn from agencies in England and Wales. I recognize that organization may differ elsewhere

and hope that readers will respond to the spirit rather than the letter
of the book.

Acknowledgements

In the interests of confidentiality I am unable to identify the many
people who shared their experience with me but I thank them.

All workers and case material have been disguised. Pseudonyms are
printed in italic. Named contributors have seen, approved and, where
necessary, revised their material.

I am very grateful for the use of the fine resources of the Brynmor
Jones Library, University of Hull. I thank Robert Holman for his
careful reading and helpful suggestions, including the idea for sum-
marizing and linking chapters, which helped to shape the text. I also
wish to thank the staff of Edward Arnold whose confidence in my ideas,
encouragement and meticulous work brought the book from my desk
to the bookshop.

I thank John Crompton for his love and typing.

'It is only with the heart that one can see rightly; what is essential
is invisible to the eye'   (de Saint-Exupéry, 1974, p. 70)

Part 1

1   How To Love A Child

Attending to children

> 'When [the children] can't stay awake, they fall asleep. If they doze off in the grass, someone will carry them home. You have wonderful faith in other people! Without that social faith, what a burden it would be to have children! The children are everyone's heirs, everyone's business, everyone's future'. (Piercy, 1987, p.183).

Direct work with children has been integral to the approach of workers in many fields for at least 200 years. The late twentieth century has seen developments in training, practice and literature.

Residential establishments preparing children for fostering and adoption have rooms equipped with sand and water, candles and paint. Paediatric wards glow with bright murals and patients enjoy well-stocked playrooms. Social workers and foster parents tackle life-story books. Family centres provide playrooms and nursery nurses. Court welfare officers and guardians *ad litem* devise means of learning the wishes and needs of children with the aid of dog-walking and doll play.

Many developments are encouraging but there are also worrying aspects. Events in Cleveland in 1988, when many children were diagnosed as having been sexually abused, led to bitter wrangling and a public enquiry exposing immense problems within the services involved, not least in communication and co-operation between such bodies as police, social services department, paediatric doctors, nurses, health visitors and voluntary agencies. Few of us could feel confident that, illuminated by that terrible spotlight, we and our employers would have emerged unscathed.

Sexual abuse is an important and distressing focus of the work of many agencies. But its significance in this book is as representative of that abuse offered to so many children, the failure really to listen, really to see and care about, really to attend.

Beatrix Campbell in her book about Cleveland, *Unofficial Secrets*, quotes Leeds doctor Michael Buchanan: 'At one time if a child said, "My dad put his hand in my knickers," people would say, "Filthy little liar." We've got countless files of children who *tried* to tell. Modesty applies – among the children and the doctors'. Doctors Jane Wynne and Christopher Hobbs, simply said: 'listen to the child, and when they say something's been in their bum they mean their bum, not somewhere else!' (Campbell, 1988, pp.22, 26).

Really listening to a child may be uncomfortable, especially if this reveals the need for such action as removal from home, or uncovers the child's fears of medical treatment or a move.

Jim (4) and *Joe* (3) were making cut-out pictures of 'the new mummy and daddy's home', as yet unknown. *Jim* said, '*Joe* doesn't want to go to that house,' His social worker, intent on preparing the boys for the move, said 'If he doesn't like that house, we'll make another one.' She recognized that *Jim* referred to himself rather than *Joe* but not until later that he meant he did not want to move at all.

Pearl Don, a social worker, had to help *May* (6) prepare for an unwanted move. The anguish of uncovering her pain and of rejecting her requests to remain in her present home was hard to bear.

Elaine Rose, with experience in a homefinding team and as a guardian *ad litem*, writing on art therapy says: 'As Social Workers, we often find it difficult to communicate with the children in our care. Somehow we feel afraid that we may damage a child by our efforts to help and that to work with a child therapeutically requires expertise. It certainly requires care, practice and understanding' (Rose, 1988, p.48).

The anxiety that we may cause damage is familiar. A sense of inadequacy pervades all work with people in need. This may be more healthy than over-confidence but it is not useful if it inhibits even trying to make contact.

The need for care, practice and understanding cannot be emphasized enough. Really to attend to children requires love and undismayed tenacity In order to face, share and alleviate the pain and often to recognize the pathetic limitation on progress while retaining hope, the worker must receive as well as give care.

Social work assistant *Kit Wells* was so nervous about life-story work with a child that he could not even begin. He had received no training before obtaining his post and felt inadequate. He drove a round trip of 80 miles on winter evenings to attend a course for foster parents and social workers where the chance to share ideas and anxieties offered desperately needed support.

Asrat-Girma studying day care for Afro-Caribbean children found that, 'many staff felt ill-prepared to deal with the problems of parents generally, and of black mothers in particular.' They 'openly admit this: "While we're on training we're nothing. But the day we qualify we're able to give advice to mothers and also be an inflated social worker"' (Asrat-Girma, 1986, p.46).

In a book review, Frances H. Smith comments on 'a sequential aspect to working with children,' that 'it does not always, or inevitably happen like this.' She had 'often gone off the rails and wondered how to get the work back on course. Where and how to pitch the work has been a recurring theme. How does the worker cope ... where the many demands of social worker/therapist can become blurred, and where such directive and sensory work can raise feelings such as anger within the worker?' (Smith, 1988, p.45).

I do not think the answer to such questions can be found in any book, any more than children's needs can be met simply by reading or drawing or playing with dolls. As children need loving contact with workers who learn each unique pattern of behaviour and wishes, problems and preferences, so workers need the attention of colleague-consultants (as illustrated in later Chapters, from the relationship between social worker Sarah Mumford and her supervisor Eva Banks).

Attending to Children cannot tell you how to communicate with *Louise* in hospital or *Nigel* in care. The aim of the book is to explore some essential aspects of working with children and to offer ideas drawn from a range of literature and from the experience of workers in several fields. This is not a 'how to' book but I hope that, as for *Kit Wells*, learning how other people feel and act will be interesting and enabling.

A Man Who Loved Children

Of paramount importance is the need to love each child. This does not mean a sentimental Christmas tinsel 'I love children' with easy substitute of puppies, Spain or gin.

It means really caring that this child is suffering, even when you don't like him much, think he has brought much of his trouble on himself, can't imagine where you'll find yet another foster home and need to get home to swallow aspirin.

It means helping her to tell you how angry and frightened she feels, bearing your own pity and terror when you tell her that she must undergo surgery, carrying your exhaustion home and smiling at her, bruised and stitched, tomorrow.

It means not hiding behind such distancing words as bonding, attachment and disruption. It means listening to the meaning behind words, finding ways, the simpler the better, to aid relaxation and communication, yours and theirs. It means facing and telling the truth and taking responsibility and weeping and aching and smiling and enjoying and loving.

An extract which haunts me illustrates shatteringly the antithesis to the work of love. It is quoted in a study *On Care of Children in Hospital*, which is based on the differing provisions and practice in nine European countries. The story, which originates with Salimbene, tells how the Holy Roman Emperor Frederik II (1194–1250) 'wanted to find out what kind of speech and what manner of speech children would have when they grew up if they spoke to no one before-hand.' Foster mothers and nurses were instructed, 'to suckle the children, to bathe them and wash them, but in no way to prattle with them or speak to them ....'

However, 'all children died. For they could not live without the petting and joyful faces and loving words of their foster mothers' (Green and Solnit in Stenbak, 1986, p.6).

June Jolly writes from experience in social work (child care) and paediatric nursing about 'a technician who loved working with the children' and 'never minded taking time to gain the child's co-operation first.' Most of the children 'came out with minute faces drawn on plastered fingertips with biro or little snow caps of cotton wool' (Jolly, 1981, p.111).

The foster mothers and nurses who should have defied the administration and given loving care colluded in the deaths of the babies. The technician who could have confined herself to efficient completion of mechanical tasks imbued even blood testing with love.

Here I must introduce a man who loved children to the extent of voluntarily dying with them in the Treblinka gas chamber.

Janusz Korczak (born Henryk Goldszmit in 1878) was Polish, with experience in education, medicine, social work and writing (both textbooks and children's fiction). The title of the present chapter is taken from his book *How to Love a Child*, (Jak Kochać Dziecko), 1929. In 1929 he also published *The Right of the Child to Respect*, (both books are quoted in Szlązakowa, 1978). 'He chose to become the "father" of the Jewish and christian (sic) children living in two orphanages in Warsaw, which he managed for many years.' He 'laid the foundations of a human existence for hundreds of lonely children in the two orphanages which, in the conditions of those times, were maintained solely by philanthropic forms of social assistance' (Szlązakowa, tr. Ronowicz, 1978, p.11).

He believed that, 'a child is often subjected to oppression from adults who think only of their own interests and comfort. For this reason, children are often "orphans in the homes of their own parents"' (p.11). He 'always emphasized the child's right to independently shape his own world and the right to human dignity.'

This is on page 12. The photograph on page 13 in the Polish book is entitled *Everyday scene in occupied Warsaw*. Two Nazi soldiers shoot through a closed house door. The horror of this archive depiction of oppression and inhuman degradation lies in the immediacy of the image. Somewhere people shoot through doors everyday.

Somewhere, everyday, in some way Janusz Korczak dies with the children he loves.

We would all give our lives for our own children. But who are our own children? Only those born from our own bodies? Janusz Korczak and at least one member of his staff, Stefania Wilczyńska, died with the Jewish orphans, refusing to desert them. 'When the turn came for Korczak's Orphan's Home the procession of children (from 7 to 18 years of age) marched in a tight formation holding high their green flag of hope. Perhaps the children thought they were going to the summer camp? Perhaps, certainly for the first time in his life, the doctor did not tell them the truth' (p.130).

Few if any readers of *Attending to Children* will be called upon literally to die with or for the children or for their beliefs. But how much will we risk? Emperor Frederik's foster mothers and nurses were surely under terrible pressure to collaborate in his evil experiment.

What do we risk for refusal to implement decisions we believe to be harmful, to collude with policies we know to be wrong? This is easier to ask than to answer and answers are easier to give in theory than to fulfil in reality.

Really to love the children may involve the loss, if not of life, at least of livelihood. There is always discomfort, always loneliness in following what you really believe to be right in the face of unsupportive if not oppressive systems, including bureaucracies of large departments and agencies. Short supply of time and money and energy can not excuse a failure in love.

Listen

Ruth Gardner, following research into the involvement of children in residential care in decision making writes that they 'are overwhelmingly the innocent recipients of what other people think, and they have trailed very poorly on the coat tails of their elders ... their "rights" to which so many adults pay lip-service, can only be realized through the willing, and at times skilled, co-operation of a carer' (Gardner, 1987, p.103).

Nicola Madge and Meg Fassam wondered, 'What does it *really* mean to be young and disabled? We decided to ask the children. Surprisingly, this is an unusual approach. Most of what is written on childhood disability is based on the observations and points of view of professionals, practitioners and parents' (Madge and Fassam, 1982, p.5).

Mary Jones and Rosalind Niblett warn that, 'children will in later life pass judgement on our decisions, decisions that they have had to live with' (Jones and Niblett, 1985, p.29).

Ruth Gardner has hopes of workers in residential establishments 'being better informed, being open to the possible value of criticism and change, gaining approval for what is helpful for children in care, and opening up better choices for themselves and others. We think there is no way that providers of services to children in care can do these things without meeting and listening to children directly' (Gardner, 1987, p.103).

June Jolly advises that, 'If we are to improve our techniques in talking with children and helping them with their feelings and experiences in hospital, there are no short cuts. We will need to be constantly on the alert, using all our skill in sensitive observation and be prepared to wait for and listen to what the children tell us. Without this we cannot hope to really communicate meaningfully' (Jolly, 1981, pp.92–3).

She adds, 'Children are almost always ready to communicate with an adult they trust. They quickly ferret out those who really care enough to listen long enough. They also need someone who will respect them enough to tell them the truth. It is essential not to laugh, dismiss or underestimate what is said, and be able to keep a confidence when asked to do so' (p.105).

Eileen Holgate, a social worker and lecturer, recognizes that 'It may be possible to make children talk, but words dragged from a reluctant, defensive child will not lead to meaningful communication. This can only come from a belief in the importance of individualizing the child and offering him direct help derived from the imaginative use of professional understanding, knowledge and skill' (Holgate, 1972, p.xv).

Paediatrician J. Apley 'had a maxim that "a surprising number of improvements in communication can be made when the doctor reminds himself that all the time he is appraising the child and parents, so they in turn are appraising him."' He also believed that, 'if a child was to become distressed in consultation ... the fault would be his. In this way he reminded his colleagues that communication was interactive, and he was responsible for getting the setting as helpful as possible to that consultation' (Wilkinson, 1987, p.67).

For caring and professional workers, really listening and recognizing that communication is interactive may lead to sharing control and thus responsibility. Lena Dominelli, a lecturer, considers that allowing 'incest victims/survivors to play the key role in developing the resources and responses necessary for reconstructing their lives becomes a positive way of empowering women and children, providing a stark contrast to their powerlessness as the abused' (Dominelli, 1989, p.306).

We who have been children must attend to the children of today. They are their own future and ours. On each small act of loving for each child fallen asleep in the grass and carried home rests the future of the world: an everyday scene of men with guns, or of human dignity?

Summary

Working directly with children is essential. This is made doubly apparent when things go wrong, as in Cleveland in 1988. Such work can be effective only if adults really listen to children, however difficult and uncomfortable this may be, and all workers should receive training, preparation and continuing support. Love is crucial to healthy development and even to life itself as exemplified in the work and death of Janusz Korczak. Extracts from writers in several fields illustrate and emphasize the need really to attend to children.

Link

Direct work with children is done every day by ordinary people in ordinary agencies. How some people approach this is illustrated in Chapter 2, whose title 'Look up from despair' is taken from the contribution of a family centre project leader.

2 Look Up From Despair

Meeting people

'How harmful overspecialization is. It cuts knowledge at a million points and leaves it bleeding'

(Asimov, 1988, p.94).

Helping children involves many agencies and workers: health visitors and foster parents; field and residential social workers; general practitioners and hospital doctors; community, nursery, paediatric and school nurses; psychiatrists and psychologists; occupational, physio- and speech therapists; magistrates and judges; solicitors and clergy; teachers, administrators and police. Workers from many settings, whether in collaboration or separately, make decisions affecting the whole of children's present and future lives.

An indispensable precondition for effective work is co-operation between adults, including of course parents.

One aim of this book is to illustrate the values, methods and problems held in common which must inform our work. Material has been collected from a variety of sources. Literature includes text books and articles referring to work in several settings and fiction for both adults and children. Material has also been contributed by workers in the agencies I visited in preparing this book or known to me in other times and places.

I had no planned programme of visits or structured interviews. I hoped to learn how individual people viewed the philosophy and practice of working with children within their agencies.

Contacts took place in a variety of ways. Usually I visited workers on their own territory but some came to me at home. The divorce court welfare officers invited me to their monthly group day where I met their guest speaker, a child guidance social worker. A guardian *ad litem* group convened during an extended lunch hour.

An exciting and encouraging aspect has been the statement and demonstration wherever I went, whatever I read, of the same principles underlying practice and the willingness to share experience, not excluding mistakes. All workers were interested in communicating across disciplinary boundaries.

This chapter introduces some of the agencies to which reference is made and illustrates various aspects of work with children. My hope is that readers will have, or make, opportunities to meet colleagues in other agencies, pursuing these introductions.

Family centres

This term is used for a wide range of projects often run by such voluntary organizations as Barnado's, The Children's Society, National Children's Homes and National Society for the Prevention of Cruelty to Children.

LADYWELL PROJECT (LP)

This was set up to work on a preventative model with families referred by health visitors or social workers as at risk of complete breakdown or with children at risk of neglect or abuse, and also to prepare assessments for juvenile court. *LP* can be flexible to meet the needs of the community.

Project leader *Ellen Barnes* regards as priority the establishment of trust. 'The majority of the families who come here have either never been loved or constantly lied to.' She aims to help families 'to look up from despair'.

Families receive help in many areas of life including domestic skills and play, 'a good way of finding out things about the children apart from the family.' It may also be the first opportunity for parents and children to play together.

ALLEN FAMILY   *Rita* was a single parent with four children, two at school. Her capability was limited and she particularly rejected *Wayne* (3) who was 'very very aggressive, not talking and naughty all the time.' Eleven-month-old *Kylie* showed signs of emulating her brother.

Work focused on helping *Rita* find better ways of coping with all four children at once, in budgeting, cooking, playing and developing her relationship with *Wayne*. *LP* worked in co-operation with the nursery, school, health visitor, social worker and department of social security and particularly aimed to help *Rita* believe in herself: she too easily said 'I can't.'

ARCH FAMILY   *Brenda* had three children under five and needed among many other things to learn to play. She talked incessantly so her twice weekly hour at *LP* was split, half for her to be with her worker, half to be with the children and play. At first *Ellen* thought the children did not know how to play but found that they could do so when given the chance.

ROWNBERRY HOUSE (RH)

This centre offers an investigation service into child abuse for a large urban and rural area, and also assessment and treatment, and training, to the whole county.

Elaine Kent and *Nancy Mint*, who are nursery nurses, regard a main aim of their work as helping children who have been abused to understand themselves. 'If you centre on the whole child she goes away from the sessions as a stronger person with increased confidence because she knows what's going on. If you centre totally on the abuse, on what actually happened, where is the rest of that child? You can give the child the impression that only the abuse is important.'

Both are very careful not to increase abuse in any way. *Elaine*'s motto is 'whatever happens I do not harm a child.' Much of their work is befriending and sharing that child's burden. 'It's very important for children to know that adults can be friends because they often become very afraid and wary of adults.'

They aim to talk to children, helping them to 'go away having got rid of fears and worries and feeling that they've enjoyed the session, had a good play.' Questions are geared to be 'revealing, not threatening'. 'Children tell you everything if you make them comfortable' but 'you've got to be listening and you mustn't be presumptuous in trying to interpret what a child says. Ask questions. Don't *tell* the children.'

RH has a well stocked play room: 'there is skill in knowing how to present a room, what to put out (and what to put away).' Although a wide range of equipment can be invaluable, 'if a child wants to tell you something it doesn't matter if the dolls' house isn't there, he'll use the glove puppets.'

Recording and remembering what children have said and done demonstrates that they are important enough to be remembered.

SELMA (6)   *Elaine's* work focused on trying to give *Selma* strategies for coping with her bizarre and negative mother. *Elaine* considered *Selma* to be emotionally abused but this was very difficult to prove. She was fine at school and in good physical health.

The fourth session was 'most traumatic' for *Elaine* herself an an unplanned and revealing role play developed. *Selma* was acting as mother to a doll, changing its nappy, cooing 'you *are* a good boy, you haven't wet your nappy.' *Elaine* asked, 'are you Mum? What would you do if he had wet his nappy?' *Selma* said, 'smack him.'

Elaine then took the role of *Selma*, who became her mother and put the doll baby in the pram to go for a walk through the playroom to a pile of teddies. Until then *Selma*/mother had been very aggressive but now she changed her whole voice and manner and asked *Elaine*/*Selma* 'would you like a present?' in a very soft stroking way. She gave *Elaine*/*Selma* all the teddies, then took her to the other end of the room

to give another, enormous bear. *Elaine/Selma* said, 'I can't carry it.'
Selma/mother immediately became annoyed, 'you will have it, I've
bought it for you.'

Elaine/Selma found the difficulty was in coping with the 'gentle mum'.
She felt frightened and puzzled; 'what have I done that's made her
nice?' She waited for aggression to return, to be punished for the
Selma/mother's being 'nice'.

Selma did not want to leave the role of mother and needed a great
deal of debriefing and cuddling, as did *Elaine*. *Selma* had enjoyed the
power and control of enacting her mother's role. *Elaine* had queries
about this work; had it been a good idea to give the girl that taste of
control?

Remaining sessions focused on anger, for example with bean bags
which represented mother, baby brother and *Elaine* herself: *Selma* had
let *Elaine* in on her world and feelings but then had to go home again
to all the real stresses. No action could be taken in response to the
evident emotional abuse; eventual reception into care followed bruising.

MAURA (13) *Maura* had 'been through hell' in a complex family in
which at times she bore most of the responsibility for housekeeping and
child care while under heavy emotional pressure. She responded to
Nancy's approaches and initiatives.

Nancy prepared numerous varied worksheets which she and *Maura*
usually worked through together. They made 'a book about me' of
which *Nancy* kept photocopies for the file. *Maura* liked to photocopy
and wield the punch. *Nancy* made worksheets and a book about herself
to demonstrate openness, truthfulness and trust in *Maura* and to have
some fun together.

Nancy was trying particularly to identify *Maura*'s feelings about her
mother using such open-ended worksheets as 'here's a telephone, who
will you ring?' She hoped for the answer 'Mummy' but *Maura* insisted
on a current pop star. *Nancy* did not press, for 'you can make a bigger
issue of feelings than the child does.'

Maura organized sessions herself, thus having some experience of the
control over her life missing at home. *Nancy* helped her to realize that
'being good and wonderful all the time could be just as bad as being
naughty and could be used as a weapon'. In the playroom *Maura* liked
playing with 'too young' toys. When eventually received into care she
blossomed, responding to the chance to play and be young, to be 'a kid
again'.

Health Visiting

Sylvia Coombes is a health visitor (HV) attached to a general practice. Most of her work is with mothers, often helping to give them 'the confidence to do what they intuitively feel is right, the chance to prove they can do well.' She doesn't 'interfere unless there's the possibility of danger.' New mothers 'often don't know what "normal" is. They compare their own children with others and then fret because A isn't doing what B does. But the range of normality is really so wide.' Mothers may also need help in recognizing being 'normally fed-up' and such illness as postnatal depression.

Work with a mother-and-baby unit in a hospital psychiatric wing may include helping mothers begin to enjoy their babies, including learning to play. 'The HV may need to give permission to play or to feel angry or not to love or like the baby.'

Sylvia considers punctuality and booking visits essential in showing respect for the families. She believes that children 'can't be conned', and should always be prepared truthfully for medical treatment and injections 'which always hurt'.

Ann Harris is a HV attached to a hospital clinic for children with special needs. Once a month three children attend for multi-disciplinary assessment including time in an observation room with a nursery nurse. Following assessment the children are reviewed periodically in clinic. *Ann* visits their homes regularly.

Although labelling can be counterproductive, she finds that it is often helpful for parents to have something with which to identify, for example, to enable them to join self-help groups. 'It is very hard for a young mother of a child who is disabled if she can see the gap between him and the development of normal children without knowing the reason why.'

Her main work is supporting parents and HV colleagues. Following the initial diagnosis, counselling is a vital part of her role. 'Once parents get over the first shock I try to help them to function as a family again.' She gives advice on development and introduces different kinds of play. Down's Syndrome children are very floppy with poor muscle tone: *Ann* may suggest putting crinkly paper (ex-biscuit tin) under limbs or tying a small bell around wrist of ankle to encourage movement and response to sound.

She suggests brightly coloured friezes and mobiles, perhaps home-made ones from wire coat hangers, with toys or pictures suspended for babies to look at and follow movement with their eyes. Stimulus is sought in every possible way, for example, babies should be put in various parts of the room to gain different sights and sounds, perhaps near windows to look at moving trees.

Ann encourages parents to put babies on the floor to develop rolling and crawling. 'Parents sometimes feel that baby walkers will get their children walking more quickly, but it is important that all children's development goes through normal stages. Walking can only happen when earlier skills have been mastered.' She teaches parents to play and sing finger and action games. Touching, holding, cuddling and talking to babies is important for them all.

Ann sometimes uses an exercise book to write ideas for stimulation between her visits. For example, for *Priscilla*: PLAY: Help her bang two bricks together. Wait to see if she does it herself. If so give her lots of praise. Play *Round and Round the Garden* ... on her hands. Sing other rhymes to her. Help her to reach our for a toy. When she has the toy show her what she has. Rattle it, help her touch it with her other hand. SOCIAL RESPONSE: When she smiles at you smile back and giver her a big kiss. LANGUAGE: Talk to her and repeat back to her any sounds she makes. Encourage this turn-taking of early communication

Ann focuses on normality, whenever possible, to help the self-esteem of parents and children. She aims for the child to achieve full potential, for the family to have the support necessary to enable it to function with dignity.

Paediatric Nursing

Anna Hughes is Support Sister, Paediatrics, in a large general hospital, appointed to work with terminally ill children and their families. She had previously nursed in a children's hospice. Much work is with bereaved children.

She believes that children can adapt to almost anything, provided that they are well prepared Explanations should be simple and factual and *Anna* considers it important to know what children have already been told. She respects parents' feelings and wishes, but sometimes finds that there are difficulties, as when a child was told of her dead mother that, 'it's magic: she's put in the box and her body goes to heaven, only the box is buried.'

Working with bereaved families includes, importantly, siblings whose needs may be overlooked. In the hospice, she says that she 'learnt so much from children' and considers her position to have been 'privileged'. The death of a child would not be hushed up, and other families, whilst showing sympathy for the bereaved, might also learn to regard the approaching deaths of their own children with less terror.

Rachel West, Senior Nurse Manager (Paediatrics), is responsible for three wards. She 'came into nursing to nurse' and retains that focus in her managerial post. The paediatric unit is small and often 'fighting for rights in a big hospital'.

Rachel regards 'all children as individuals, even the premature babies. I don't see children as mini-adults,' Much of her work focuses on reducing fear and anxiety in both children and parents. To help hospital become as much 'a fun place' as possible the wards are full of bright paintings and murals, posters and toys. The trolley used to take children to operating theatre is decorated as a Postman Pat van with headlights and 'the children have fun from it, as we do.'

Children who have been injured non-accidentally place considerable strain on staff who may need help with their feelings. A student nurse had felt antagonistic towards a father who had severely injured his child; however, when she met him 'she felt only pity'.

The death of a child, whether as a baby or from disease or accident, has a great impact on staff who feel and share grief with bereaved families. Support and understanding is needed for all levels of staff in these and other situations.

An important focus for both *Rachel* and *Anna* was the establishment of access for children, accompanied by a familiar adult, to the intensive care unit (ICU) to see severely ill parents and siblings. Resistance often came in the form of 'they'll get too upset', but experience gained from many cases has shown that children do benefit.

Anna prepares by, for example, showing photographs of the ICU, including the ventilator, so that they will not be horrified or distracted by the reality when they see it. She also uses a doll equipped with tubes and bruises which can be adapted to resemble the individual patient. She explains how the patient will look, saying, perhaps, that the daddy they will see will be the same daddy they know, although he will look different, for example with his hair brushed back.

She recalled a girl who had thanked the ICU staff, and later told *Anna* how important it had been to say goodbye to her mother. 'I know she's better off now. She wouldn't have wanted to be handicapped.'

Children are encouraged to talk to and touch unconscious parents and siblings and are helped to conquer their own anxiety and distress to find ways of communicating. *Bob*, who was gravely injured and, although conscious unable to speak, comforted his deeply distressed sister by holding her hand and nodding. Assured that *Bob* was alive and recognized her, she could also find comfort in noticing how much of her brother was uninjured and normal.

Recognizing normality was also important to such children as *Jenny*, whose sister suffered from a progressive degenerative disease. Visiting the hospice, *Jenny* could learn from other children that she was not the only child with a handicapped sibling.

Probation Service

DIVORCE COURT WELFARE

The divorce court welfare service is staffed by seconded probation officers, styled court welfare officers (CWO), whose duties include reporting to court on possible orders and provisions with respect to custody, access, care and control or education.

CINDY (5)   *Cindy* lived with her mother but her father had applied for custody. Care in both homes was even. *Laura Bridge* needed to learn *Cindy*'s wishes and feelings without direct questioning. She had met *Cindy* in both homes. Final contact took place in the probation office, an informal and neutral setting with toys and pictures.

Cindy was invited to make a bus from lego, choose who would travel on the bus and make three wishes. She elected to have the bus driven to the seaside with her mother as the sole passenger. The second time *Cindy* chose to share the driving with her mother, parking the bus at home beside a toy car representing her mother's VW.

JED (8)   *Jed*'s mother had taken him to live far away from his father, to whom she was very hostile. In order to advise the court about access arrangements, *Laura Bridge* supervised *Jed*'s visits to his father.

Laura arranged a meeting with both parents and a male colleague, *Rod Pine*, to discuss the importance to *Jed* of access visits. The presence of a male and a female CWO is often arranged for joint visits, to provide balance and support.

Jed was not present at this meeting but afterwards, as part of the plan, *Laura* and *Rod* spent time with him on his own. *Jed* already knew *Laura*, from her attendance during access visits, but he had never before seen *Rod*.

At once, he showed great interest and paid particular attention to the male worker. For example, whenever *Rod* spoke to him, *Jed* cupped his head in his hands and gazed at him.

Laura had already considered that *Jed* was very happy to be with his father. Also, the father was important as a role model; (there were no other males in *Jed*'s immediate family). Seeing his father infrequently had, perhaps led to some idolization, far from the effect the critical mother had intended. During the joint interview *Jed* said, 'I think he tries very hard.'

The joint interview, and *Jed*'s response to *Rod*, confirmed *Laura*'s impression that contact with his father was of very great importance to the boy.

CARA (11)   *Cara*, subject to contested access, came on her own initiative to the office telling the secretary that she hadn't told anyone about this. She had not seen *Rod* alone before. *Rod* was out and pondered how to proceed without betraying her. He wrote apologizing for having been out and asking *Cara* to call again but to ask her mother to telephone and make an appointment. She did return. *Rod* believed *Cara* felt she had been recognized, being of enough importance to be sent a letter.

KEN'S CASSETTES   When contact between parents has broken down *Ken Brent* suggests that cassettes may be used where telephone or face to face meetings are impossible. He helps fathers make tapes and can assure mothers and children that 'what's coming is completely safe'. Children often want to keep the cassettes and listen again. A tape can focus 'on the fun side. Letters, telephone impose questions which children are expected to answer. Tape doesn't.' One father put the pets on the tape too; the cat can be heard purring louder and louder.

One mother refused access but the children were allowed to listen to their father's taped voice. After seven months they would race to put the tape on. When mother saw this she agreed to access. Another father sent a beautiful half-hour tape about his journey to Scotland and life there without the children. While listening one child held his mother's hand, the other her foot and all visibly relaxed. The tape could be stopped when they felt too emotional. Mother and children prepared a tape in return.

PROBATION

Alec Grant is a probation officer fulfilling a large range of duties in a probation office attached to a court covering an enormous rural area with a few small towns. His work with young people under 18 is mainly focused on writing social enquiry reports (SER) for the magistrates court and implementing supervision orders (SO).

ART (16)   *Art* had been made subject of a one-year supervision order following an offence. He had spent a period on remand some way from home where *Alec* had visited him while preparing the SER. He had been able to make some practical contribution to the boy's welfare, for example, providing a new pair of socks, and he had helped *Art* obtain bail.

Alec experienced considerable difficulty in making contact with *Art*, who could sit indefinitely in uncommunicative silence. After four months *Alec* noticed an improvement in body posture (he said, 'I spent a lot of time looking at *Art*'), and *Art* began to respond by smiling once or twice.

Art's mother took an interest in him but discipline was left to his father whose work took him away from home a great deal. Father either 'took no interest or was reluctant to be disciplinarian so nothing happened,' which appeared to indicate to *Art* that there was no sign of interest; 'discipline can indicate that there is care.' *Art*'s male role model was either remote and distant, or threatening and negative. His father said 'I can't do anything with him.' So *Art*'s experience with *Alec*, of a man taking a benign interest in him, felt strange.

Alec could not be confident that *Art* would not offend again or that there would be much progress during the life of this SO. But he thought that *Art*'s 'smile may be a hopeful sign for next time. He may not be ready yet but respond more later.'

BOUNDLESS PROJECT Much work with young offenders is undertaken within groups. The *Boundless Project* organized by *Nick Bright* aims to aid personal development, growth and effectiveness. Activities cover a wide range including music and mountaineering, 'anything they can succeed at', and are arranged to encourage development in motivation, responsibility, experiential learning, planning and accomplishment. 'You can't fail on the group, learn by mistakes. If you find a new skill you must be able to show off.' *Boundless* members may go hillwalking, potholing and white water rafting and join two-day residential adventures which include hiking, cycling and canoeing. They take responsibility for all planning, including budgeting and buying and cooking food. The adults define achievable aims.

Social Work (Field)

CHILD GUIDANCE

Helen King is a senior social worker at a child guidance clinic. Much work is 'looking at what part parenting plays in disturbed behaviour and assessing the capacity of parents to meet a particular child's needs.' This includes compiling a three-generation story.

About a quarter of her work is with children of warring or divorced parents. This may involve arranging joint access which 'can exhaust the workers'. Social workers may invite warring parties to their office where 'they act as referees, providing a lot of coffee. No one really wants to see you and contact may feel imposed. The impact of such work on the workers is tremendous. We need resources, training and support.

'Parents may use children manipulatively, for example, "She can't come, she's got a cold" or in trying to prop up a dead marriage.' About 15 per cent of referrals are of children displaying behavioural problems arising from access arrangements. Yet they may be labelled as having psychiatric problems, referred to a child psychiatrist and identified as such on the general practitioner's list.

Working with children is constantly a matter of 'using what comes to hand. You have to tailor your approach to the child, think what the child would like to do.'

PATTY (6)   *Patty*'s father had died suddenly after sexually abusing her. *Helen* saw the girl in the clinic playroom working to help her recognize and express her feelings. One day *Patty* filled with sand a length of plastic hose from a toy hair dryer, then spilled it out of the hose. She played this 'ejaculation' many times, almost wearing out the hose. Helen offered this as an example of using materials that come to hand. She could not have planned that the hose and sand could be used in such a way but she did notice and respond accordingly.

BRUCE (2)   *Bruce* was bedwetting, pining, moping, not eating and screaming 'don't make me go'. Far from being 'disturbed' his distress appears to have been a reasonable response to his twice a year fortnight-long visits to his father several hundred miles from home. *Helen* focused on improving access arrangements to four week-long visits a year. Although this eased the immediate strain *Helen* feared future problems.

RHONA (8)   Following her parents' divorce *Rhona* was placed in a private boarding school. Neither parent could provide even a regular holiday home. School, where she was very bright, was the only place where she felt safe and had any sense of achievement. However, she was soiling and smearing. With *Helen* she drew angry pictures of blood and daggers. *Rhona* had no other way to express anger with her parents. Her surface behaviour was always charming and polite. Seeking ways to make contact and learning that *Rhona* liked backgammon, *Helen* brought her own set to the clinic. However, *Rhona* compared this unfavourably with her own set, which was never available to bring to the clinic: it was always in one or other of the parental homes, or at school, but seemed never to be in the place where *Rhona* needed it. *Helen* thought that this might mirror *Rhona*'s lack of control over her own life.

GUARDIAN *AD LITEM*

Guardians *ad litem* (GAL) are qualified social workers appointed by courts to work on behalf of children involved, for example, in care proceedings.

CATHY (15)   Following alleged sexual abuse by her stepfather *Cathy* was placed in a residential home. When *Stella Hill* first visited, *Cathy* was hunched up staring at the floor. *Stella* tried to reflect what she thought the girl would be thinking: 'you don't look as if you'd want to talk to me. You'll be thinking I'm yet another one who'll get you to talk and then go away.' She stressed her neutrality and that she was on

Cathy's side, not the parents' or social services department (SSD) or police.

She explained who she was, including some personal information. As a student she had been taught not to do this but 'you wouldn't tell a blank wall your innermost secrets!' Clients are helped by seeing 'you're prepared to give a bit of yourself.'

Cathy felt that she was being punished for something she hadn't done by being removed from her own home and kept in a 'quasi-remand home', In addition she was included in a general punishment within the home imposed for a misdemeanour perpetrated by someone else. She was very angry with her stepfather and the SSD.

Stella 'had to work to the girl's agenda' before she could begin on her own. She gained *Cathy*'s confidence and was able to recommend a supervision order and return home. 'Various people did believe her so that she had protective mechanisms to fall back on.' Further stay in care would be less than conducive to *Cathy*'s welfare. However, a care order was made and *Stella* appealed on behalf of *Cathy*. She lost but within a few weeks *Cathy* had been placed home on trial.

During the year involved *Stella* gave *Cathy* 'a lifeline out of the residential setting and probably saw her more than her own social worker.'

AMY (5)   *Fran Trent* visited *Amy* in a foster home, where grabbing a toy telephone, *Amy* pretended to call her mother and said, 'I don't want to see you anymore.' She was safe to speak so, yet the toy gave the fleeting illusion of really giving her mother this difficult news.

JERRY (5) and *LOUELLA* (2)   Both children were in care following alleged cruelty to *Jerry* by their mother. *Megan Lewis* visited them in the foster home, with their mother, and at school/nursery. At *Jerry*'s school she was given the resources of a whole classroom. *Jerry* organized a little girl to bring in a pot of paste, dismissing her when her service was complete, despite her clear wish to join the party. He cut out figures of family members and other significant people, sticking them on a sheet of paper as close to or distant from himself as he thought appropriate. He confounded *Megan* by placing his dog nearest to his own figure.

The court returned *Louella* home partly because of *Megan*'s calculation that the months already spent in care comprised an eighth of her entire life and that prolonged separation from her loving mother was in itself more harmful than the remote possibility of physical injury.

SOCIAL SERVICES

Sheila Galleon has experience in a number of social services departments (SSD) including a family placement unit (investigating applications for fostering/adoption and arranging placements).

She considers it essential to combat the 'lives in slices' and lack of 'continuing thread for children in care'. This includes helping both children and foster parents after 'disruption' which leaves 'a great gaping wound.' Both parties need release from guilt 'to see that there were good things,' for if no help is offered 'they can only see it as all bad.'

GARY   Sheila advises about 'the need to find the child's medium, what they are comfortable with, their level of understanding, what are their interests?' *Gary* had been in care since babyhood with numerous unsuccessful attempts at rehabilitation. At 10, *Sheila* began to prepare him for 'permanent' placement. His present home was not happy because of rivalry with the foster parents' own son *Rory*, also 10.

Seeking to engage *Gary*'s interests *Sheila* recalled his passion for football. She explained that the foster family had two centre forwards and thus the team could not win. *Gary* needed to be in a team where he could be the only centre forward. *Gary* responded to this idea and was helped successfully.

PETER   Sheila herself had experience as a foster mother. When *Peter* moved to a 'permanent' foster home after a substantial stay with her family, she asked his social worker to tell *Peter* she was asking about him. The social worker refused 'because it would upset him.' *Sheila* considered that 'it would have been important for *Peter* to know there was continuity.'

Lives in Slices

A Guardian reporter spent a day with some social workers:

> Sue is steaming. She puts the phone down and leans hard on the desk, controlling her anger. A woman has abandoned her new-born baby at hospital. The hospital wants the baby moved, because they need the bed. Sue Harris, duty cover at a social services office, is trying to arrange an assessment of the mother's mental health. She wants the GP to visit the mother, with a social worker. The GP doesn't seem to want to know.
>
> 'The doctor is going round in 15 minutes and does not want to get involved with mental health problems . . . .'(Boseley, 1990.)

Social worker Clifford Parris, with two midwives, eventually gains entry to the mother's flat, just too late to see the doctor. The mother 'is 26, but looks like a sad, defenceless child.'

Lack of co-operation, if not overspecialization, may leave not only knowledge but children, their families, and caring adults, bleeding.

Summary

Co-operation between the many workers and agencies who may be involved in influencing and intervening in the lives of children is essential. Short descriptions of some approaches to working with children are drawn from contacts with practitioners in several settings, illustrated by references to children and families. Particular points emphasized are the needs to:

- ensure training, preparation, support and resources for staff.
- encourage both children and adults to develop confidence and self-esteem.
- attend to each child individually and to adapt both approach and equipment accordingly.
- develop continuity for children whose lives are dislocated.
- regard the whole child, rather than focusing on symptoms or problems.
- develop co-operation and understanding.

Link

Working with children inevitably brings adults into contact with pain. Part 1 of this book has introduced some ideas and individuals concerned with such work. Key words are listen, love, wait, co-operate, and these are as relevant to contact between practitioners as to that with children.

Part 2 studies particular aspects of the work: the first topic, often neglected in text books and practice, is about endings, including loss, death and move of home; the second topic is a consideration of beginnings.

Part 2

3 Beginning with ending

The cost of concealment

Every beginning follows an end. To have been adopted or in permanent care children must have experienced the end of life with their birth families. Some children suffer the death of one or both parents following accident or illness. Emotional tasks are about surviving shock, recognizing and bearing loss, and developing a changed way of life with the surviving parent or a new family. Adults often hide fear of their own feelings behind 'concern to protect children from distress'.

When *Roy* was 12 his father *Frank* developed inoperable cancer. The consultant advised *Roy*'s mother *Jean* not to tell the boy, although *Frank* was to spend the last months of his life at home. As *Frank* died by appalling inches in his own sitting-room, *Roy* was officially ignorant of the impending death.

As *Frank* grew weaker *Roy*'s treasured birthday present alsation puppy grew stronger. One morning, while *Roy* was at school, a kind neighbour removed the puppy to another home. *Roy* was never consulted although the dog had been his own.

On the morning of *Frank*'s death *Roy*, in ignorance, was sent to school. When he came home his father had disappeared for ever.

Two years later *Jean*, who had never recovered from tearless depression, also died from cancer and *Roy* was taken to live with relations whom he hardly knew. Overwhelmed by her own fear, anxiety and grief *Jean* was never able to acknowledge that her son might experience such emotions himself. When she was dying in hospital *Jean* allowed *Roy* to visit her only with extreme reluctance. She was prepared to disappear too.

Roy's behaviour was unchanged by the disappearances of dog and father. He showed no surprise or grief and pursued his life at school and with friends, obedient, pleasant and placid. Because he expressed no feelings, it was assumed that he had none to express.

It is often tempting to believe that children have no uncomfortable feelings, that resilient implies untouched. Moving children around like parcels protects the adult from the full force of unbearable emotion. Workers are rarely provided with either time or personal support to bear the impact of a shocked and grieving child.

Patricia Goldacre, teacher and educational therapist, worked with a five-year-old girl who 'failed in her fostering (with a view to adoption) after her foster father died suddenly at home one evening. She became obstinate and restless, refusing to stay in bed at night, and disordered in her language, so that her foster mother felt she could no longer cope with her.'

To find out if she was mentally handicapped 'She was sent to an assessment centre where, after many months of activity in the classroom, the child, who was now clearly seen to be of above average intelligence, said to her teacher, "They think I don't know what happened the night my father died, but I do know, I heard it all, I was awake and went out on the landing."' All the problems 'became explicable in terms of the circumstances of the foster father's death, the failure to discuss it in rational terms with or in front of the child, and of course the subsequent rejection of the child by the foster mother' (Goldacre, 1980, p.37).

Saying Goodbye

Saying goodbye is essential to any future healthy hellos. Alfred Torrie, a general practitioner and child psychiatrist, and husband of the founder of Cruse, wrote of 'The four-year-old who wanted to go to Great Grandma's funeral service yet said at its end "Mummy, why didn't Great Grandma come?" "She did ... she was in the box." The child said no more, but later at intervals, came more questions' (Torrie, 1978, p.11).

A funeral may provide much good for bereaved children to use later. *Fergus* and his mother were with his father when he died in hospital after a long illness. His younger sister *Beth* had been staying with relations but she was taken to see her father in the mortuary. At the funeral the children mixed with many friends and relations, exchanging hugs and tears, and seeing and hearing evidence of the high regard in which their father was held and the care people felt for them and their mother. This was continued by the display of the many beautiful flowers and wreaths at home and the memorial fund for their father.

Parents of babies who die in the special care unit in *Rachel West*'s hospital are encouraged to stay with their babies, to visit the mortuary as often as they wish and to share their grief with staff and other mothers. Similarly, mothers whose babies are awaiting adoption placement are welcome to visit at will, preparing to say goodbye.

An important time for saying goodbye is at the end of a placement in an adoptive, foster or residential home. Workers may achieve strong relationships which, hard to establish and costly to maintain, may too easily be concluded without recognition of their importance to all concerned. Social worker Elaine Rose, a guardian *ad litem* with experience in art therapy advises, 'Never underestimate the value of your contact with the child. You may be the first person to have given the child a feeling of value in his or her creative pursuit. If you terminate your art work ... without due attention to the separation processes involved, you will undervalue yourself, the child and the insights gained for you both' (Rose, 1988, p.50).

Concluding intensive work, social worker Andrew Small recognized his 'need to grieve the loss of Jason.' The ending of the work was marked 'with a celebration at the Centre when the goodbyes were said', including a ritual with candles which 'demonstrated to Jason that the love and warmth he felt for earlier carers did not have to be "blown out!"' (Adcock, Dubois and Small, 1988, pp.132–3).

Saying goodbye on returning home from hospital or care is important too for both staff and children, but in their study of children *In and Out of Care* Mike Fisher and colleagues found that, 'In general, the process of ending care was not accorded much attention by most social workers. On the whole, their accounts of ending care were much less detailed than ... of entry into care' (Fisher *et al.*, 1986, p.114). They quote a mother who 'described the process of ending care as something that professionals did with minimal family involvement.' She said ' ... all of a sudden social worker come and said that you can have her home or they'll send her to ... is it a remand centre or somewhere, they'd send her somewhere, but you could have her home, just like that and I can't understand it to this day why.'

Her daughter described the same event thus, 'It were about half an hour before I came home they told me I'd got to put my stuff and that ....' The children's home 'phoned my mum and dad and then half an hour after that they told me to go home and I'd got half an hour to pack all my stuff and staff were just chucking stuff in bags' (pp.106–7).

Fisher and colleagues consider that, 'If the provision of care is going to be a constructive part of the solution to a family's problems, and if it is going to be focused on the prevention of permanent family break-down, then discharge from care must be an important ingredient of the overall provisions of help' (p.136).

However much planning is advocated for entry to or move within or from care, Jane Aldgate and David Hawley felt, 'concern that seven children from our small sample were moved without much preparation or involvement of their foster parents.' Frequently, 'the children were collected and taken away, occasionally by a strange social worker, sometimes at very short notice, a process which seemed to offer the worst of all possible worlds for everybody concerned. Children reacted to their rejection with distress or surface indifference and foster parents with devastation' (Aldgate and Hawley, 1986, p.46).

They quote a foster mother: 'I just phoned up at the end of my tether for my social worker but I couldn't speak to her so I let out all my feelings on whoever was there. And the next thing was that Barbara just went, I wasn't expecting this – they came to collect her. I felt it wasn't working out – we just didn't get on but I didn't expect her to go like this' (p.47).

Precipitate and damaging moves are not confined to the care system. *Anna Hughes* had been horrified when despite all the efforts of herself and *Rachel West*, *Kirsty* had been transferred from intensive care to join her brother *Ellis* in the paediatric ward. They had planned to prepare both children for the move, for *Kirsty* was in traction and her face badly bruised and swollen. *Ellis* was still very ill himself and coping with the news of his mother's death. The ill-judged move caused increased stress for both children.

Goodbyes may be said prematurely. *Vicky* (16) was preparing to move from a large community home to a hostel where she looked forward to having her own room and increased independence. She packed all her belongings, including an enormous bean bag and a table lamp, said goodbye to her colleagues and, in the sitting room with her keyworker, *Gill* awaited the social worker *Rex*. Rather late *Rex* arrived and, greeting *Vicky* in passing, asked *Gill* to accompany him into another room. *Vicky* was stranded with her luggage and no clue what was happening. Eventually *Rex* informed *Vicky* that there was not after all space for her at the hostel. 'Her' room had to be used for someone else. *Rex* departed and *Gill* was left to help *Vicky* unpack, difficult, but even so the easiest task in a day which had started with goodbyes and would end with embarrassed reunions. *Vicky* dealt bravely with all this, helped tremendously by *Gill*.

What have I done to deserve this?

Children entering care can rarely be prepared because admission is usually during or resulting from a crisis which inevitably ends part of their lives. Whatever has led to admission, the child enters a nightmare: sudden removal from parent/s, physical examination, maybe admission to hospital, rides in cars, placement in a strange house with strange adults and probably strange children, possibly a new school, appearance in court, other people examining, asking questions. Parent/s, brothers, sisters maybe visiting the new house or seen at an office or in the court building. Complete loss of grandparents, friends, pets.

Tracy (6) and *Lyn* (3) were removed on place of safety orders because their father was alleged by a neighbour to have hit *Tracy* with a belt. *Lyn* was taken from home, *Tracy* picked up from school with no opportunity to say goodbye to her parents. *Tracy* was bruised but not badly injured and both girls had a strong attachment to their home. They remained in care for several months, comprising a sizeable portion of their short lives. This point made by the guardian *ad litem* helped to secure their return home subject to supervision orders.

Precipitate removal by social workers (unknown to the children) and length of separation from parents could have been more damaging than physical injury inflicted by their father. Scarce resources might have been better used in helping the family instead of expensively keeping the children in care and exacerbating the problems.

Sometimes removal from home may have for the children no obvious connection with any problem. What can they make of sudden separation from parent/s? How are they at fault? What have they done to deserve this punishment? *Sally*'s father *Les* committed a sexual offence against his niece. After his prison sentence he returned home with the consent of *Sally*'s mother *Rene*. *Sally* was removed and eventually made subject of a care order.

Sally saw *Rene* regularly in the community home but was to be allowed to see *Les* only in the social services department under supervision, which he refused. *Rene* constantly promised *Sally* that she could return home soon but refused to separate from *Les*. *Sally* must have felt responsible for her removal and punishment, an appalling retribution for what crime?

Jane Aldgate and David Hawley comment on rejection experienced by children whose placements are disrupted, reinforcing the sense of badness common to many children in care. 'This low self-image is bound to be battered even more by the disruption but the effects can be ameliorated firstly, by honest and open discussion between families, social workers and children about why things have gone wrong, secondly, by allowing children time to meet new carers and thirdly, by involving old carers and their family in the move to the new placement' (Aldgate and Hawley, 1986, p.46).

Often sudden removal follows a history of abuse and assault: physical, emotional, sexual. Relief at the ending of torture combines with guilt, anxiety, loss and shock. However bad the status quo, sudden change in which we have no say and over which we have no control is terrifying. However jolly the foster dog where is the homely labrador? What has happened? What have I done? Children received into care or moved between foster or residential homes may attribute these moves to their own naughtiness, whatever the true cause.

Prevention is certainly better than cure. Cure that does not recognise itself as major surgery is perilous, even emotionally lethal. The social worker's knife may be wielded in order to begin a régime of new health and fitness but the children are usually unwilling 'patients', not consulted, unprepared, unanaesthetized, severed from their families without warning, the wound uncauterized. Surely they are better off away from the awfulness, the abuse, better off in a good clean loving foster home: better off, maybe, but amputated.

Adjusting to loss

May the children, relieved of unsatisfactory parents, grieve? May they show bewilderment, fear, loss? Will they be taken seriously for missing not mother, it seems, but personal stereos, for asking to see not father but the hamster? Do big boys cry? Or do they tuck into sausage and chips and 'settle very well' with some television Soap?

For caring adults it is usually most comfortable to believe that children have settled well, whatever the setting. Jocelyn Maximé in her study of black children in care found that, 'Most black children in this society are reinforced positively when they show signs of adjustment to and acceptance of society and its values. This happens even when society is so often hostile and rejecting to black people.' Cherry (10) had lived in a children's home for nine years. She 'was described as a "well-adjusted obedient little girl who will fit nicely into a family." '

However, the social worker found her difficult to assess and considered that she had 'difficulties in self-acceptance. Cherry spent much of her time in a make-believe world producing beautiful paintings, all of white people. Furthermore, Cherry insisted that she wanted a white family as black ones were all too poor.'

Jocelyn Maximé undertook further assessment and 'discovered further that she refused to interact socially with black children and denied the label "black." ' Her 'rewards came clearly in the form of favourable description of her behaviour and an acceptance of her as a "well-adjusted" child. Here we have a black child described as "well-adjusted" but unable to accept herself and hold positive feelings about herself.' She was clear that Cherry 'was not "well-adjusted." How could she be when she disliked herself?' (Maximé, 1986, pp.102–3).

Cherry, like many other children of whatever colour and background, was expected to say goodbye, to end the part of her life which preceded her role as a child in care. Approval, even survival, depended on the conviction with which she could play that role and appear to separate herself from her past. But the past is the present and the future.

Once, in my service as a child care officer, I remember a good reception into care because the child himself chose to go. *Mark* (9) had spent a few weeks in care following some out-of-control behaviour leading to a supervision order and return home. He knew the benefits of residential life: television, pocket money, no shouting, restricted chores. At home he was dogsbody and scapegoat. At school he was blamed for every offence, whether innocent or not. Never given the benefit of the doubt, he added to his animal attributes and decided it was as well to be hung for a sheep as a lamb.

Life at home became intolerable. Sitting on the stairs in the hall we decided together that he would like to move house. Alone.

This led to a good ending to precede his chosen new beginning. The whole family calmed down and enjoyed a peaceful, even happy weekend together before *Mark* left home with dignity.

Although *Mark* and his family never again lived together they were able to maintain good images of one another. When *Mark* went home for a holiday his father accorded him the rare honour of opening the front door and appearing in his best trousers.

The child removed suddenly from home in inexplicable and worrying circumstances is caught between the experiences of *Roy* and *Mark*. *Roy* and other children whose parents die suffer the ultimate, total loss; the dead parents can never come again. *Mark*'s parents were alive and available but safely under control.

For children like *Sally* the parent is and is not, living but lost and surrounded with confusing emotions and events. The child is expected to form attachments to new parents while knowing perfectly well that her own are in good health, have decent accommodation and say that they wish her to live with them.

How can you mourn someone who is still so much there? And how really make a new beginning in a new home without thoroughly leaving the old one?

Others have to bear the unbearable knowledge that their parents have disappeared altogether or, though with a known address, wish to have no contact with their offspring. They may even continue to produce new babies. Dead but not dead, for reappearance is always possible. So how to mourn? And how to help the child mourn? Easier to say 'better off without them' and ignore the child's unexpressed pain. Easier to regard the child as well-adjusted.

George Eliot captures the pain of childhood loss and adult defence in *The Mill on the Floss*:

> We have all of us sobbed so piteously, standing with tiny bare legs above our little socks, when we lost sight of our mother or nurse in some strange place; but we can no longer recall the poignancy of that moment and weep over it as we do over the remembered sufferings of five or ten years ago. Everyone of those keen moments has left its trace and lives in us still, but such traces have blended themselves irrevocably with the firmer texture of our youth and manhood; and so it comes that we can look on at the troubles of our children with a smiling disbelief in the reality of their pain. Is there anyone who can recover the experience of his childhood, not merely with a memory of what he did and what happened to him, of what he liked and disliked when he was in frock and trousers, but with an intimate penetration, a revived consciousness of what he felt then – when it was so long from one Midsummer to another?
>
> (Eliot, 1979, p.63).

Else Stenbak writes of the movement of bewildered children through 'protest, despair and denial'. A child experiencing denial looks cheerful and interested in the environment and seems very happy when relating to staff, but really cannot 'Bear the painful fact of losing his parents and prefers to ignore it' (Stenbak, 1986, p.8).

Patricia Goldacre links the feelings of children who have lost parent/s through death and by 'divorce, abuse or inadequacy'. But, 'For children who are old enough to understand the permanence of death as against the possibility of reunion when death has not occurred, there are important differences which workers must not overlook.' She considers that 'In the case of separation as a result of divorce, the child can overcome feelings of rejection and guilt by having access to the absent parent .... When there is no access children feel continuously rejected and permanently guilty if they know that the absent parent is "out there" somewhere.'

It may be possible to reduce but not eliminate 'feelings of rejection and guilt following separation and loss ... by including children, especially older ones, in the making of plans for their future. Without this, children assume that they are being rejected because they are bad.' (Goldacre, 1980, p.40).

The loss of parent/s may be effected by the caring workers and agencies themselves, for example, by removal from home. John Pierson, a senior training officer, comments on a decision to terminate parental access to children in care. He refers to a case study in which contact between a father and his daughter in care was 'finally severed although he had great affection for her, visited regularly and was reasonable in behaviour. Moreover, he recognized he could not care for her himself. But the professionals involved saw him as "interfering" in day-to-day matters and unable to understand his daughter's need for "security and stability" with her "substitute family".'

He suggests that, 'parental behaviour must be seen to be concretely damaging to the child's emotional life over a lengthy period of time to warrant severing contact permanently' (Pierson, 1989, p.42).

Helping with endings

Helping children to acknowledge and deal with loss and endings cannot usually be completed before the fresh start, for the end itself necessitates an immediate beginning, entry to care or hospital, a move to live with relations, or life continuing at home lacking a parent or sibling.

Three essential and fundamental ways of helping are telling the truth, acknowledging and expressing one's own feelings and helping children to acknowledge and express theirs, and maintaining attention to everyday needs and routines.

Truth

In her study of bereavement in childhood Erna Furman found that, 'it was much easier for the child to comprehend death factually when it was not initially associated with the loss of a loved person and, by the same token, it was easier to understand the death of a loved one when the child already had a concept of death.'

Susie (3) asked, soon after being told of her mother's death, ' "Where is mommy?" Her father reminded her of the dead bird they had found and buried not too long ago. He explained that mommy, too, had died and had to be buried. He would show her where whenever Susie wished.' A month later Susie said that a boy had told her, ' "mommy would come back soon because his mommy said so. I told him that's not true because my mommy is dead, and when you're dead you can't ever come back. That's right, daddy, isn't it?" '

The case material illustrated how 'children attempted to come to terms with the reality of their loved one's death and how meaningful and helpful concrete evidence of death was to them at certain points.' In contrast, this task was made very difficult 'when the adults in their environment wittingly or unwittingly misrepresented or obscured the objective facts' (Furman, 1974, p.50–1).

Alfred Torrie shows that 'Unrealistic explanation about death – that it is merely sleep or that the person had gone away – apart from being untruthful, can lead to sleep disturbance and anxiety reactions about journeys.' (Cf. the little girl who refused to stay in bed at night after her foster father's death: p.27). 'The child may fear that the traveller will be "got at". A widow told her children that Daddy had gone to the seaside. She feared telling the truth so told a lie. To re-tell the story could well disturb her children's faith in her' (Torrie, 1978, p.7).

Lying to children is not only demeaning but also wastes opportunities for growth, even in death.

Feelings

Helping children acknowledge and express their own feelings may be very painful for workers, including foster families. Jane Aldgate and David Hawley quote a foster father: 'Foster children are your kids too while they live with you and it's a year out of their lives, so it must mean something to everyone.' They comment, 'Not only do the parents in the family need help but ... the own children in the foster family may be left with a similar residue of feeling to that experienced by their parents. They too often need help in their own right ...' (Aldgate and Hawley, 1986, pp.49, 47).

Eve (7) and her time-limited foster family became very attached to each other. She asked to stay permanently and all the family members went through several weeks of soul-searching (literally, for they had a strong religious faith). After much pain and with deep regret the parents realized that they could not offer a permanent home. On one visit by *Eve*'s social worker, *Abby* (12) said simply 'I love *Eve*.' The family recognized that the greatest service would be to provide loving bridging placement, facing the grief all would have to bear when she eventually left.

Often the caring adults need to support one another. *Jim* (4) and *Joe* (3) were in a time-limited foster home awaiting placement for adoption. Their social worker *Joan* visited weekly to develop a life-story book, help final separation from relations and prepare for placement. When the boys became upset they were cuddled by *Joan* and *Maria* the foster mother. *Jim* continued to be upset all day.

Joan felt upset and guilty and found it difficult to begin work the next week. She and *Maria* agreed to keep such safe topics as a photograph of the foster parents but at the end of the session *Jim* himself asked to make a man doll (from a toilet-roll cylinder), 'the new daddy' which had been suggested at the end of the previous session. *Joan* and *Maria* supported each other during this distressing period. The foster family cared deeply for the boys and felt great loss when eventually they moved.

Aldgate and Hawley advise that it is 'important for former foster children and their families to be given some post-placement contact to lay the ghosts of misunderstanding .... Own children of foster parents should be included in these visits because they may have worried about what has happened to their friends' (Aldgate and Hawley, 1986, p.48).

Jane Aldgate regards caring and empathy as part of being professional. 'Because experiences of loss are universal, seeing children in distress may evoke recollections of workers' own experiences. Some of these may not have been resolved; they may get in the way of work with the child unless they are confronted and examined in supervision' (Aldgate, 1988, p.47).

After the very distressing disruption of a placement I broke down and wept in the open-plan team room. My senior officer at once cuddled me. Colleagues left us space but I felt surrounded with their concern and was soon fortified with coffee. Although I still feel scarred the healing of the care for me is strong too.

In the hospital setting *Rachel West* said: 'Children may die here. This has great impact on the ward.' She takes care to talk with staff and both the bereaved parents and parents of other children on the ward, *Rachel* herself found the stress of a particular situation, with complex family politics raging over a sick child for many weeks, exhausting. Her own senior officer offered much support and her colleagues expressed concern.

David J. Müller, Pam J. Harris and Lesley Wattley advise nurses to 'recognize their own and each other's emotional needs and take positive steps to ensure that these are being met' (Müller *et al.*, 1986, p.204).

Writers too need to recognize the impact of their material. While engaged in intensive visiting and reading and particularly when focusing on death, I became exhausted and depressed; I felt surrounded and oppressed by pain. I was reading a collection of children's books about dying parents and friends, thinking that I could skim through these with impunity. I was also working with some children in care which I found rewarding but very demanding.

At last recognizing that I must have a break (if only for the sake of my husband) I understood how foolish I had been to imagine I could distance myself from the pain of the children about whom I was learning and with whom I was working. A relation younger than myself had died recently and my feelings about this were constantly reactivated. All this resonated with my own fears of loss and illness. Only the patience and support of my husband rescued me.

There is emotional cost to the supporting person, too, whether spouse or supervisor. Sarah Mumford worked with John (4) whose mother had died. She and Eva Banks consider that 'Supervision is essential in enabling the worker to cope with the intensity of the feelings raised, for example, by working with a bereaved child. If Sarah had not used supervision in this way she might have become overwhelmed. Eva was aware of the risks of exposing inexperienced workers to such powerful feelings' (Banks and Mumford, 1988, p.106).

The work with John was helped by their willingness to face the truth with him, and by a bag of dolls, 'We felt that he needed to know the facts – that the hospital and the doctors had tried to make her better but that she was too ill.' When Sarah told John he 'began to enact the scene at the hospital with the "doctor" doll operating on the "Mummy" doll. When the "doctor" doll "failed", ... it became the object of all John's anger, and he would receive severe reprimands for not making people better.' John would give the "doctor" doll a punch in the face or bash its head on the floor' (1988, p.105).

Alfred Torrie considers that 'It is difficult to know when a young child can fully understand what is told him, but it is important to give the child an opportunity repeatedly to talk about the event, to ask questions about it, to describe his own ideas of what may have caused it and to express all his feelings.' Even 'If the small child cannot understand fully, nothing is lost; if he understands only a small part, much is gained' (1978, p.8).

With Margaret (14), whose brother had died of a drug overdose, Pat Goldacre found poetry the catalyst. Margaret had not been 'allowed to see her brother's body or go to his funeral. Her behaviour deteriorated and this led to her reception into care. She was a clever girl of whom much was expected.' Daily, she began an essay which described 'My Family' as ' "my mother, my father, my two older sisters, my younger brother and my younger sister." This was the composition of her family *now*, leaving out the brother who had committed suicide. It was a way of telling me about it but I decided that I would never refer to her loss until she could tell me more directly.'

Margaret's behaviour was very disruptive. Eventually Pat Goldacre read two poems, one being Rupert Brooke's 'The Soldier'. 'Margaret let me read both these poems through without interruption because her attention and silence were gained by mention of a young man who had died ... The unmentionable had been mentioned....' Margaret asked the worker to take her to the cemetery saying ' "I *had* a brother, I expect you know. He's buried there. I wasn't allowed to see him or go to the funeral. They wouldn't let me though I asked. Could we go there?" ' On the way there and back she told me much about her former life when her brother was alive. The barrier was broken. Memories of her brother were once again bearable' (Goldacre, 1980, pp.39–40).

Routine

Most important to children is normal everyday life. After crisis, whether entry to or discharge from hospital or care or the divorce or death of parents, children need the re-establishment of routine. Disruption of this may have more impact on the child than the crisis itself. When her father is dying in hospital in Jean Little's story, Sarah becomes anxious because she 'thinks she can't come home for lunch even if she wants to' (Little, 1985, p.68). She can't, because her mother is visiting the hospital. The routine of family life is already broken forever.

When *Paula* (12) was placed for adoption with *Miriam* and *Andrew* who were vegetarian, they provided her with meat for as long as she wished in order to maintain as much as possible of her former everyday life.

Patricia Goldacre writes of the 'value in holding onto everyday routine activities, including school. In the continuation of everyday living and striving life goes on, grief gives way to comfort, the comfort of creating, satisfaction in learning and in achievement' (Goldacre, 1980, p.40). 'All children', she says, 'need to feel valued....' The quality of everyday, everyminute communication must enhance, or destroy, that sense of worth essential to healthy life.

Only if caring adults can face the implications of endings with children, can they help beginnings to be positive and healthy.

Summary

Concealment of, for example, the pending death of a parent is dangerous and denies both children and adults the opportunity to recognize and share such feelings and experiences as grief and anxiety. Saying goodbye may facilitate future healthy beginnings and development. Preparation for endings is as important as for beginnings. Children who suffer, for example, removal from home and moves within care, or the divorce of their parents, may experience anxiety, bewilderment, sense of badness, guilt and loss. Adults may misinterpret apparent lack of distress or discomfort as good adjustment. Children need to express and receive recognition and acceptance of their true feelings, however uncomfortable for adults. Helping children to acknowledge and deal with loss and endings entails attention to truth, feelings, and re-establishment and/or maintenance of routine.

Link

Endings and beginnings overlap all the time, Workers hoping to develop a relationship with children or, for example, helping children prepare for a move or medical treatment, need to be aware of what is finishing and the implications and impact of new people and events. Some of these are explored in Chapter 4, 'Begin at the beginning.'

4 Begin at the beginning

A magic carpet ride

From the *Hull Daily Mail*, 21.03.90:

> Jean's magic carpet ride has, over the years, helped many children confront and escape from the horrors of a life of physical or sexual abuse.
>
> Hidden away in one of her cupboards Jean, a Child Protection Officer with the NSPCC, keeps a small rug. The rug is shabby and worn but to an unhappy and confused child it becomes magical.
>
> Jean starts by asking the child to join her on a magic carpet ride, lays it on the floor. She then sits on it cross-legged and asks the child to join her.
>
> She tells the child that as long as they are on the carpet their words cannot escape or be overhead, no matter what they say. No-one will ever hear them or know they exist.
>
> At the end of the session the carpet is rolled up very carefully and carried to the garden where Jean and the child unroll it to let all the 'words' blow away
>
> (Halliday, 1990).

Beginning contact

For many workers contact has to be made quickly and frequently with scarce opportunity for meetings. Health visitors see young children in clinics and at home. Assessments are made at various ages. The health visitor needs to attract the child's confidence quickly. *Sylvia Coombes* asks mothers to prepare children by saying that she will be coming to play some games. She always sits on the floor and makes the various tests fun.

Social workers and probation officers have more time to make assessments and formulate recommendations to court. Even where the law or individual courts allow a generous period for investigation it is necessary to work quickly in order to reduce the suffering and anxiety of children waiting in limbo.

Making contact and developing a relationship can be difficult, particularly if the worker feels pressure to obtain information quickly, not least in order to protect the child. There can be conflict between trying to work at the child's own pace and completing a report. But it is surely wrong to expect any child to confide in a stranger.

Particularly sensitive is disclosure work following alleged abuse: physical, sexual or emotional. Moira Woods, a doctor in Dublin, waited 18 months for an eight-year-old girl to tell her about abuse by her father (indicated by her wide vagina and dilating rectum) (Campbell, 1988, p.33). (See also Chapter 8.)

Yet children may wish to talk at once. Moira Woods recalled a little girl who 'was four days in hospital with vaginal bleeding, looked at by four doctors. I asked her, "What are you in hospital for?" and she said, "My bum is bleeding." I asked, "What made your bum bleed?" and she said, "He stuck his willy in my bum." Nobody had asked her' (p.32).

Divorce court welfare officer *Laura Bridge* said, 'Some children are bursting to talk to you, may be only too grateful to talk to you.'

To develop skills of waiting and demonstrating readiness to receive whatever children wish to communicate requires really paying attention. It means putting the child first, recognizing that there may be such internal pressures as trying to obtain information too fast in order to prove oneself to be a successful communicator.

My worst session with one child preceded a case conference. I was so determined to contribute immediate information that I failed really to attend to the child; during the meeting I could remember hardly anything of the session concluded only an hour before. I had been too keen to be seen as doing a good job.

Trying to begin a more open-ended relationship may be difficult too. Sarah Mumford became 'depressed and despairing ... convinced she would never get anywhere' with James (13) who, 'had been in care nearly all his life and had had numerous changes of placement. He was an unhappy child who looked and behaved much younger than his age. The staff at his children's home found him hard to understand and difficult to contain.'

With a fortnightly visit Sarah 'found the task of developing any kind of relationship with him almost impossible.' James 'would rarely look at me or say anything and was always firmly ensconced in front of the television as soon as he was home from school' (Banks and Mumford, 1988, p.108).

Elaine Kent and *Nancy Mint* have given much thought to first impressions and beginning relationships. They introduce themselves using first names and sitting on the floor. They indicate to the child, 'I'd like to learn all about you,' but avoid pressure. Children are bound to feel anxious about attending the family centre, 'they know there's something special. The aim is for them quickly to feel comfortable and by the end to feel free of fears and that the session has been enjoyable, "a good play!"'

Selecting equipment for a session becomes easier as workers and children get to know one another. For the first meeting a variety of things are displayed and the first two or three sessions are devoted to play, to enable 'trust building and confidence, leading towards talking about family members.' They 'give openings from the word go, for some children may want to talk at once.'

The equipment may 'allow openings'. *Cassie* (5) was a very difficult child even before her sister accidentally drowned in her presence. For the next session *Elaine* put out clay and a bowl of water but did not direct *Cassie*'s attention to this. *Cassie* dunked all the clay saying, 'I'm drowning the clay.'

The manner of beginning contact anticipates the whole relationship. Focus on the whole child instead of symptoms, whether abuse or illness, loss of parent or need of a new home, is itself crucial to healing.

Children should know the boundaries of contact and expectations, both their own and those which they may meet. These include limits on activities, for example avoiding physical injury, and on time.

Beginning work with *May*, *Pearl* set a firm limit of one hour. When *May* was facing painful memories *Pearl* allowed sessions to run on. Meetings took place in the foster home and one afternoon the foster mother called to say that tea was nearly ready. *Pearl* realized that her thoughtlessness impinged on the whole family, not least because she and *May* used the sitting room. After this she adhered firmly to the time limit and found *May* responding to the need to choose activities to fit in with the time available.

Children need to know that there is a limit on the intervention, whether pleasurable or painful. They also need to be sure of their full quota of time and attention. Punctuality at both beginning and end gives an important message of respect for the child. *Elaine* and *Nancy* expresses this as 'the child needs to know that for that hour he's the most important person in the world. If the child is kept waiting the message is "am I important if I have to wait?"' Expecting to begin a session at a certain time and then being kept waiting can result in the child 'going off the boil,' starting delayed contact with negative feelings.

When the appointment causes anxiety it is common to imagine that by X o'clock it will all be over. 'Think of me at three o'clock,' you say hoping for some magic to reduce the ordeal. If by four o'clock you are still waiting, the strengthening thoughts have been used up and the anxiety (including the need to pee yet again) is rocketing.

One effect of unpunctuality on me is to become ruthless about the other people in the waiting room. Now I want my full quota of time and attention even though the designated finishing hour is past. I feel angry and jealous of the person who has kept me waiting and the client/patient who preceded me. The precious structure of 'my' time has been demolished.

Fear and anxiety

When children are subject to examination and assessment, not only is contact with an unknown adult potentially frightening but there is also inevitably anxiety about the outcome. Even if a child is not spontaneously anxious, parents communicate their own fears.

Physical examination may follow such frightening experiences as accident or assault and may itself become part of the horror. At the Dublin Sexual Assault Treatment Unit Moira Woods and her colleagues, '*looked* in every child'. Some 'would tell you that he stuck something in their bum. But a lot of them, the very frightened ones, won't tell you anything. We looked because we were not going to miss *anything*. And children aren't going to tell you, a total stranger, everything on the first interview. Of course they're not: why should they?' (Campbell, 1988, p.32).

The setting for such an examination may well be frightening however many bright murals and toys fill the clinic. Social workers often have more choice of venue. Divorce court welfare officer *Elsa Gray* took some warded children on whom she was to prepare an assessment on the suitability of return to a parent, to her own home for a day. All day they played cards, made drawings, devised a family tree 'and nothing came out. Then at the end the children poured out everything' that *Elsa* needed to know. 'The important thing is to create the right milieu; car journeys can be useful.'

Laura Bridge takes children for walks with her dog: 'If they don't tell me they might tell the dog.'

Guardian *ad litem Fran Trent* finds glove puppets useful in engaging children's interest. She pulls *Goldie* from her handbag while talking to the adults so that the child can approach and show interest without immediate direct contact. When the child begins to show confidence *Fran* may say for example, 'You tell *Goldie* what it's like living in this house.'

Be at ease

The most important single factor stressed by almost all the workers I met is that both worker and child should feel at ease. It is no good playing with glove puppets if you feel silly or walking with dogs to whom you are allergic.

Solicitor Mike Morris writes about aids to communication including 'The fifth and final device' which 'is not one I have ever tried, but I have listened to others who have, and who speak glowingly of its virtues; activity-based communication. Sport, for example, either by participation or watching, can apparently create a bond which produces communication hitherto unheard of. It is not my style ...' (1986, p.55).

Sport was not the style of social worker *Lyn Verrall* either, but she took *Colin* (14) to the city football match Saturday after Saturday, gradually gaining his confidence, their relationship growing warmer as her feet froze.

Children should be able to reject proffered activities and indeed any help at all. *Christa* (15) concluded two sessions with *Elaine* saying 'I'm here because there's a problem; I think it's more my parents' problem.' *Cathy* (15) threw the *Anti-colouring Book* (Striker) back at her guardian *ad litem, Stella Hill*: 'what do you think I am, a kid?' *Stella* and *Cathy* were able to build a relationship with no aids to talking and listening.

Elaine and *Nancy* emphasize the importance of 'following the child's lead. You have to listen to everything. A child may have made small comments several times during a session or may return to some comment in subsequent sessions, dropping hints.' This may include 'giving permission to be four or five if that's how they feel, to be silly.'

Honesty and plain dealing

Beginning work with children requires honesty, explaining the reason for the contact and what the child may expect of the worker. Probation officer *Alec Grant* compiling social enquiry reports (SER) for court, focuses on the event of committing the offence rather than the offence itself.

He begins contact with separate letters to the boy (usually) and parents explaining why he is making an appointment. At least one parent or guardian must be present but *Alec* asks permission to see the young person alone at some stage. He is conscious that family members feel anxious and confused. He aims to arrange at least one interview in the office and one at the boy's home.

He tries to 'set the stage by explaining who and what a probation officer is, the purpose of a SER and the client's rights.' He also explains that the boy has the right to read and to challenge the SER in court. He prefers to go through the report in draft, considering that a typed version may appear too final and difficult to challenge.

A 'stock response to "why did you do it?" is "I was bored." It takes time to reach a more personal explanation of the event.'

Ellen Barnes and her colleagues make 'time limited agreements with families giving details of when they are to come, what is expected, what they want, who's going to be working with them. Their link worker (the keyworker is always a social worker) is responsible for the work, including monitoring the file, but others may help, perhaps because of some particular skill. Work is usually at the family centre, though some may be transferred to the family's home.

'All family circumstances are different. We try to meet their needs in ways acceptable to them; then there's more chance that they'll come!

Some work is extremely intensive and very personal. The families need to know that space, that worker, is *theirs*. Families do open up, and sometimes tell things you'd rather not know!'

The children are usually very young but they are part of the agreement. Such an agreement made directly with children themselves can give a clear focus and form to work, demonstrating respect and confidence. This applies to medical assessment and treatment as much as to work in the fields of social care and welfare.

June Jolly is convinced of the importance of telling children the truth. 'One child commented, "They said it wouldn't hurt – only because it doesn't hurt them. They don't know how it feels" Many of us say these things because, frankly, we hope it won't hurt. We dislike the idea of inflicting pain and tend to deny its existence' (Jolly, 1981, p.97).

She remembers a six-year-old whose mother had said that the doctor would remove his tonsils 'with a special sort of spoon – near enough to an accurate description for me to use in future preparing of children. This child was also told the doctor would give him a "magic sleep" first, which he obviously thought would be fun' (p.98–9).

Müller *et al.* advise that 'there are no events in hospital which are routine to a child or parent who has not been inside a hospital before ... preparation does not need to be elaborate, and ... information alone, pitched at the right level and presented in a sensitive way, is very effective in reducing the distress of young patients and their parents.'

They warn that 'Many parents and children do not ask questions because they perceive the staff as too busy' and 'it is important that information is provided even when it is not requested.' When 'staff make the first move, the way is then opened for discussion of the concerns of individual children and their parents and nurses can correct any misinterpretations ...' (Müller *et al.*, 1986, p.123).

Preparation

In *Will This Hurt?* Jocelyn Rodin describes research into the efficacy of preparing children for medical procedures through a study of preparing children attending their local clinics for blood tests. She concludes 'that children benefit from being prepared for a medical procedure, becoming less anxious and more co-operative than children who are not prepared ....' In addition 'this beneficial effect was increased appreciably if the parents had already told their children something about the procedure beforehand and warned them what to expect.'

Possibly, 'increasing benefits might have been observed if the parents had used this material beforehand with their children' for 'such use could alleviate the parents' own anxiety and so contribute further to a reduction in the child's anxiety ... the anxiety shown by the children was clearly and directly related to the anxiety shown by the parents' (Rodin, 1983, pp. 89, 82, 90).

Rachel West considers that 'we underestimate their powers of understanding' and that children respond very well to preparation for medical treatment which usually ensures 'no screaming habdabs'.

To help combat fears children booked to undergo ear nose and throat (ENT) treatment are invited to attend the ward on Saturday morning. They see a video and play with gowns and masks, 'have time to adjust to the ward and meet the staff.' The children usually head for the delights of the playroom leaving parents to discuss anxieties with staff.

Rachel finds that 'parents still tell children such untruths as "you'll be home tomorrow."' When staff have to correct these, children may be angry with parents for misleading them. It is important to acknowledge in advance that treatment processes will hurt. The ENT video, for example shows an 'anaesthetist who asks the child if she has a cat at home and says that he is going to scratch her like a cat. The picture goes disturbed like a dream just as it does as the anaesthetic works and the child goes to sleep.' When the children are admitted on Monday morning they are relaxed; 'For example, they know where to wee.'

June Jolly describes 'a "preparation for operation" book ... with a three-dimensional aspect. Little flaps over the masked faces of the attendants, nurses and doctors, when lifted, revealed their normal smiling faces. Similarly the sheet could be lifted off the theatre trolley. You could see children found it reassuring to discover the patient was still whole' (Jolly, 1981, p.103).

Else Stenbak considers that 'it is important for a child to be assigned to a special person. To express anxiety, a child or an adult needs to feel emotionally safe.' Children should also 'be allowed to bring ... toys, clothes or other personal articles' (Stenbak, 1986, p.17, 56).

A vivid example of the importance of good preparation is given by June Jolly about a boy (7) 'with an unstable fracture, who had been transferred to us from an adult ward', and 'was acutely anxious. Unfortunately, having waited all day to go to the theatre, he was finally called in a hurry and there was no time for adequate premedication. By making sure he was accompanied by a senior nurse, whom he trusted and who had in fact prepared him, he was anaesthetized without distress.' This nurse 'had showed him some plaster of Paris and then let him soak it and put it on a doll's leg. He watched it get hard and talked about how it would come off, he soon considered himself the ward expert on his own plaster cast!' (Jolly, 1981, pp.99–100).

Children awaiting cardiac surgery were helped by nurses performing a very simple demonstration game 'on a rag doll'. When the children 'regained consciousness in the intensive care unit, the dolls were on the pillow – as directed. Some of the children projected much of their feelings on the doll "models". Others seemingly forgot about them until the time for the removal of sutures' (p.100).

Preparation for some specific event or treatment may be relatively straightforward aided by concrete information and visible equipment. Certain routines can be anticipated, including physical pain, nausea, weakness and recovery.

For children involved in choice between parental homes and access arrangements, anxiety and distress may be tempered with the retention of familiar people, places and possessions. Children entering or moving within care face less tangible challenges or threats.

Helping children to know and face truth is essential but the truth of being unwanted by not only your own parents but also, it seems, a succession of foster parents, or learning that your mother has AIDS or your father sexually assaulted you or that you have an incurable disease cannot be turned into 'fun' as can playing cardiac operations with rag dolls. After the operation the rag doll is sitting on the pillow and convalescence may replace pain. Scars left by terrible truths faced by children and their workers are more than skin deep.

A new place

Admission to care is an end to ordinary life. Ordinary life for a child in care in Great Britain may imply residence with one or two foster parent/s and usually not more than two or three other children. The other children may not all share both parents but they are probably related to one or the other and are thus half- or step-siblings. The family probably occupies a house or flat with one living room, a small kitchen and two, three or four bedrooms.

Children needing reception into care often enjoy far less space, for example, sharing a bedsitting room with parent/s and siblings. Children entering care are likely to come from families with very low incomes. Their homes may lack such mechanical aids as washing machines and vacuum cleaners, thought by most of us to be essential.

Adcock, Dubois and Small recommend that children, 'whatever their age, need to know beforehand that they will be going away from home or moving to another placement. Repeated explanations and discussions enable information to be absorbed, reducing the risk of misperception and misunderstanding, and helping to diminish the feeling that 'it must be my fault''' (Adcock *et al.*, 1988, p.124).

Once in care children may undergo a number of moves when, except in the most unavoidable emergency, there should be no reason not to undertake preparation work. My double negative demonstrates ambivalence about this statement. Field social workers frequently find themselves unable to fulfil this kind of work, usually because their departments are so crisis-orientated. But such work need not take a great deal of time and must surely help to prevent future crises.

If the child has a good start in this foster home this time, is there not a better chance of the placement succeeding? And does not that have important implications for the child's future mental and emotional, and indeed physical health? Money is spent to prevent physical illness, why not to aid mental and emotional health?

Workers at the Family Makers Homefinding Unit, Gravesend, describe the project as child centred. It 'aims at involving the children at all stages from a planned period of introduction to the unit through to eventual placement in a new family ...'. New methods of direct work are developed 'with children helping them understand the moves they have experienced in the past. Individually designed games, puppets, plays, tapes, life-story books and videos are all explored as potential aids' (Connor *et al.*, 1984, p.44).

Each child 'is assigned a keyworker' and 'encouraged to explore his own feelings about families and staff work hard to develop the child's realistic and positive expectations about living in a new family.' This is 'painful and demanding work for staff and children' and 'it cannot be assumed that theory and practice will magically coalesce unless staff have necessary skills, enough time and imaginative training and support' (p.45).

A detailed account of preparing children for a fresh start in a new foster home is given by Lily and Albert Foreman. Many simple devices are employed to accustom three young children to the idea of moving and to facilitate the first meeting with new foster parents. The children had been told that Mrs Peters had a red dress, which she thoughtfully wore.

'The children set out three small tables, one for each child. Then they picked flowers from the garden to put on the tables, then biscuits, cakes, drinks, and all the children's favourites. ... When they arrived all the children ran to greet them. Cheryl ran up to Mrs Peters and said, "Hello, Mummy Peters, you are wearing your red dress." '

Through play with paper houses and cardboard people, the foster family helped the children work towards the move. 'We started by getting them to put everyone in their own houses. Then we would all go to tea in the Peters' house. For about a week we all always ended up in one house together. We could not get them to divide us up. Mark would put Jerome and Cheryl with the Peters but he would always stay with me in our house.' However, 'After a few weeks of visits in these paper houses we managed to get where we should be.'

When their social worker had introduced the idea of moving 'All the children were angry and hurt each other.' A great deal of sensitive, unobtrusive and co-operative work converted the anger to a happy move. 'The parting was easier than expected and they all went off happily. I had to reassure them again and again that we would always be here.'

Ten months later the Foremans could report that the children were happy. An ending had become a healthy beginning (Foreman, L. and A., 1985, pp.54, 55, 57).

Summary

Beginning to make contact with children may need to be done quickly. Although some children may wish to talk at once, it is always essential to wait until the individual child is ready, which may take a toll of the worker. The manner of beginning anticipates and is crucial to the whole relationship. Setting boundaries on, for example, time, choosing equipment, being punctual, focus, setting, – all give important messages. Examination and assessment stimulate fear and anxiety. Both children and workers need to feel at ease in their contacts and to undertake only activities with which both parties feel comfortable. Honesty and clear explanations are essential from the first moment of contact. Preparation is always important and can help children, for example, undergo medical/surgical treatment, and moves within care.

Link

Part 2 has explored some aspects of helping children experiencing endings and beginnings in particularly stressful situations. Part 3 considers some philosophical, ethical, emotional and spiritual issues.

Part 3

5   From fear to trust

Fear

What are you afraid of?

Adults in western society fear a great deal. Although in 1990 the threat of nuclear holocaust seems less than even two or three years ago we are caught in a web of fear for the future of the Earth, woven from the destruction of rain forests and the ozone layer, the interactions of chemicals and foodstuffs, animal and vegetable, and the effects of industrial waste and accident – nuclear, chemical, oil. Not only humanity but the whole Earth is under threat.

We fear to travel on the London Underground after murder, mugging and rape. We fear for the safety of ourselves and our families, flying, driving, crossing the road. We fear to be burgled, to lose our jobs, our money. We fear illness, age, death.

The worst responses to fear are paralysis and panic, flight reactions to crisis, implying failure to confront problems and to use courage and common sense. People intent on spreading information and raising awareness about the effects of nuclear explosions found that pictures of dying children and lectures about global disasters could drive us into personal bunkers of don't-make-me-know-it's-too-horrible-to-bear. A peace group I knew promoted the benefits of peace, instead of publicizing the horrors of war.

Fear, like all emotion, must have some positive function. Fear of destruction by the unbalancing of the atmosphere and exploitation of the Earth has led to such groups as *Friends of the Earth* dedicated to conservation, and an understanding of our individual contributions to pollution. Fear of lung cancer may deter some people from smoking. Fear of being burnt may prevent rather more from clutching fire.

Trust

It is usually better to be motivated like the peace group by more positive aims than the avoidance of personal suffering. 'Lead me from fear to trust' says a Peace Prayer adapted from the *Upanishads*. Trust by the time we reach adulthood may be hard to sustain. Many experience betrayal: infidelity by a partner, rejection by teenage offspring, broken promises by colleagues, disappointment when expensive goods fail to resemble glossy advertisements.

Adults who survive and thrive emotionally avoid paralysis or panic and continue to risk trust, both giving and accepting.

It may be difficult for adults to develop and maintain trust. It will be all but impossible if trust has never been developed in childhood, indeed from the moment of birth.

Eric Erikson's (1956) model of human development identifies 'Basic Trust' as the first essential stage on the long haul towards maturity. It is widely held that a child who is prevented from that first achievement in relationship will be inhibited from positive emotional development, unless and until provision of an environment in which trust can be established. A child who has been betrayed may have great difficulty in trusting again.

How soon do children lose the innocence of trust and learn to fear? My husband John remembers the fear of losing his mother, from the age of three. He had spent some time apart from her so that fear was based on experience. He 'remembered' the separation as lasting for a long time although in reality it was only a few days.

I remember that fear, too, and had occasional separation dreams well into adulthood, my mother lost in a shop or busy street. But I was apart from her for no more than a few hours at a time until I was six and always if not with her in the care of a loved grandmother.

John, who had fallen out of many trees by the age of 13, when he broke his arm, never feared either climbing or falling. I, inhibited from either climbing or falling by 'don't hurt yourself', feared both and am still a coward.

I describe these personal memories because I think one of the best ways to understand the fears of children is to reach back to our own. We all as children feared different things but there are common elements.

Of God and goblins

A friend recalled that, after her son's first two attendances at Sunday school, she found him in bed completely covered by the sheet. He said 'If God is everywhere, can he see me here?' The fear of God had become not reverence for divinity but terror of an omnipresent monster. A boy (4) 'had great difficulty in falling to sleep after his father died. He demanded that all the windows be kept locked ... he was unwilling to cross streets or be out of the shade of trees. The mother had told him that God had reached down from Heaven while his father slept, had picked him up and taken him to Heaven' (Torrie, 1978, p.7).

Another friend, *Ena*, spoke of her daughter who had for three years demanded a light in her bedroom to keep at bay the old women who, with other unwelcome night visitors, came in through the window. She had no clue to the stimulus of this fear or why it ended.

Fear of the dark and its inhabitants is common. Children's books often describe exploring in caves and surviving the menace of unseen assailants.

Much of *The Princess And the Goblin* is set in the halls and galleries of a great mine. The reader shivers in fear as the Princess and Curdie encounter malicious goblins. Through Curdie the reader can dare the intolerable. 'He was most anxious to get back through the hole before the goblins should return.... It was not that he was the least afraid of them ...' (MacDonald, 1871, p.92). Maybe not, but I was, in words and pictures. I hid behind Curdie and followed him as in pitch darkness he

> hurried on, feeling his way along the walls of rock. Had he not been very courageous, he must have been very anxious, for he could not but know that if he lost his way it would be the most difficult thing in the world to find it again ... [Eventually] he found his way blocked up, and could get no farther. It was of no use to turn back, for he had not the least idea where he had begun to go wrong.
>
> (pp.92–3)

Curdie in deep darkness has no fear; he is in control of not only himself but also his environment. He can mine-read using senses other than sight. Much fear derives from the sense of helplessness, The dark may be frightening because the loss of a sense, sight, destroys the balance of the light-seeing self.

Is not the core and basis of all fear that we find ourselves in situations we cannot control? We fear the unknown: the dark, the monster, the old women crawling in at the window. We fear also the known: repetition of experience already suffered. John feared separation from his mother because he already knew how that felt. We fear pain because we have felt pain and did not like it.

My monster myself

Ena suggested that children's fears are different from those of adults. Is this true? Adults are children who have grown older and I have deliberately not discussed the chronological ages of children relative to experience and feeling. My feelings depend on and have developed from those of my childhood. My fears at nearly 50 relate to those I had at five: loss, separation, pain. The difference is that adults should have more resources with which to combat fear, more experience and cognitive range and more control, if not over the threatening events and circumstances, at least over their own responses and behaviour.

In many children's books and most westerns and war stories, heroes confront clearly identified problems or enemies, showing immense courage and winning. In *A Wizard of Earthsea* Ged flees from the terrible monster he has, as a trainee wizard, unleashed:

> Through the bright misshapen breach clambered something like a clot of black shadow, quick and hideous, and it leaped straight out at Ged's face. [He] fell, struggling and writhing, while the bright rip in the world's darkness above him widened and stretched....
> [Only his friend Vetch stays,] So only he saw the lump of shadow that clung to Ged, tearing at his flesh ... Vetch sobbed with horror, yet he put out his hands to try to pull the thing away from Ged. Before he touched it, he was bound still, unable to move.
>
> (LeGuin, 1971, pp.74, 75)

The familiar paralysis of fear, of the dream in which you can't wake up, can't lift your arms, can't scream.

Ged runs from the terror for years until he recognizes that only by subduing his own fear can he escape. He turns and hunts the hunter. At last, when he ceases hunting and learns to wait, he and the shadow meet.

> Aloud and clearly, breaking that old silence, Ged spoke the shadow's name, and in the same moment the shadow spoke without lips or tongue, saying the same words: 'Ged'. And the two voices were one voice. Ged ... took hold of his shadow, of the black self that reached out to him. Light and darkness met, and joined, and were one.
>
> (pp.197–8)

When he believes that he has no control Ged runs from the menace which is itself the uncontrolled part of himself. When he masters his fear he masters too the cause of his fear. But Vetch can only watch from a distance in terror and later with an anxious dread.

Dumb, numb and hopeless

I'm the King of the Castle, a novel about two boys, is pervaded by fear, a nightmare of children forced into unwanted proximity because Kingshaw's mother has become housekeeper to Hooper's father. Through external events their internal terrors are revealed. On an outing to a castle Kingshaw confidently climbs ruined walls. Hooper, terrified, remains on the ground until taunted, he begins to clamber and becomes paralysed. Kingshaw returns to Hooper 'sure of his own judgement. The only thing was not to rush.... Hooper did not move. Kingshaw looked at him closely. His face was green-white' (Hill, 1974, p.151).

Kingshaw takes control:

> 'You haven't got to look down, you've got to look at your feet and think about what you're doing.'
>   Hooper opened his eyes and at once, his gaze was drawn towards the

ground below. He said, 'Oh God ...' in a whisper, and shut his eyes
again, screwing them up hard, until his cheekbones rose. He had not
moved his body at all.

Kingshaw noticed the dark, damp stain of pee in the groin of Hooper's
jeans. After a moment, drops of it came trickling down his leg and fell
on to the stone on top of the wall....

He would have to be terribly careful not to say or do anything to
frighten him.

Kingshaw reached out his hand. In terror, Hooper flinched and took
a step backwards, swayed and fell.

(pp.153–4)

Hooper is also terrified of thunder storms to which Kingshaw is
indifferent. But Kingshaw has his own terrors including moths (dead
and alive) and crows. He is chased by a crow which actually lands on
his back. 'He lay and closed his eyes and felt the claws of the bird,
digging into his skin, through the thin shirt, and began to scream in a
queer, gasping sort of way' (p.32).

Many more terrible events demonstrate and reflect the core of Kingshaw's fear.

He knew that there was no hope, ... He did not attract luck to himself,
he attracted un-luck. Bad things happened, not good things, and it
didn't make any difference what he thought or felt or did. He felt more
than afraid. He was dull and numb, with the reality of it....

(p.61)

Dull and numb; how many children are described thus? 'He doesn't
show any feeling, she's very withdrawn, they'll settle anywhere, children
are very resilient.'

May (6) had four foster homes in three years. Her fourth placement
finished because the foster parents found her unresponsive. There were
fears that she was withdrawing into a world of her own, spending hours
in her bedroom and having little or no idea about the world around
her and her own life and history. *Pearl Don*, asked to help bring her
back into touch with 'reality', began to make a life-story book with her
and discovered that two previous books had been started. She saw this
as a symbol of *May*'s life, constant fresh starts without connection. The
books were even kept in different places.

May's life-story books symbolize reality. Susan Hill's novel represents
the reality of Kingshaw's life, that he has no security because his mother,
when 'she looked at him, ... did not understand .... She had never
known anything about him, he had never wanted it' (p.62). Plenty of
people, social workers, foster parents, teachers, looked at *May* and
wanted to understand. Like Kingshaw, she desperately needed her fear
to be understood for however much Kingshaw did not want it, he was
certainly in need, such need that he eventually killed himself.

Having no-one to trust, Kingshaw has no confidence in life. His physical confidence on the castle walls was a kind of challenge, a game of control. The terror of birds and insects was of external, alien forces, uncontrolled because moving without his control and associated with death. Hooper too is afraid of death and falls because, when he is forced to trust the person of whom he is most afraid, he cannot relinquish control and so loses control.

Betraying adults

At one point Hooper locks Kingshaw into the dreadful Red Room in which, he tells his victim, his grandfather had died. Kingshaw's terror there mirrors that of 10-year-old Jane Eyre similarly confined in a Red-Room, death chamber of her uncle. Terrified of ghosts,

> My heart beat thick, my head grew hot; a sound filled my ears, which I deemed the rushing of wings; something seemed near me; I was oppressed, suffocated; endurance broken down; I rushed to the door and shook the lock in desperate effort.... [Mercifully before long] I suppose I had a species of fit: unconsciousness closed the scene.
>
> (Brontë, 1966, pp.49, 50)

a scene so terrifying in its direct connection with the real fears of childhood that my husband, who had recently taught a course on the Brontës, confessed to having lost consciousness of it.

For me the most fearful aspect of that scene now is the behaviour of the adults who confine the little girl and respond to her cries of terror with punitive suspicion.

> She screamed out on purpose.... If she had been in great pain one would have excused it, but she only wanted to bring us all here; I know her naughty tricks ... [and] you cannot succeed in getting out by these means, be assured. I abhor artifice, particularly in children; it is my duty to show you that tricks will not answer; you will now stay here an hour longer....
>
> (p.49)

What chance for Jane to move from fear to trust when 'caring' adults interpreted terror as artifice, the very terror which they had deliberately induced and fostered? Perhaps this reaches us more closely when interpreted into those familiar terms, 'she's only attention seeking' and 'he asked for it.'

Kingshaw's mother and Jane's aunt are responsible for the appalling development of fear in the children because they hear and see only what they choose; Helena Kingshaw regards her son as 'settled down so happily'; Jane is condemned as 'not worthy of notice, ... a compound of violent passions, mean spirit, and dangerous duplicity', 'a responsibility that was becoming too irksome' (p.67).

The extracts about Hooper, Kingshaw and Jane illustrate a number of phenomena associated with fear, including such failures of control as running, shouting, involuntary micturition, loss of consciousness and paralysis. Frightened children cling to adults, burrowing, clasping, hiding. Running, they have someone to run to; fearful, they have someone to trust. For Kingshaw and Jane no-one is trustworthy. When they run it is *away*, seeking only freedom from fear, expecting no comfort.

Children run away literally and emotionally, Lacking the safe haven of a trusted adult world, perhaps betrayed by the very adults they should have most cause to trust, they may cease to waste energy on the outward signs of fear and of frustration and bewilderment, and like *May*, retreat.

More than the kiss of a fairy-tale prince is needed to call an emotionally hiding child out from the safe hedge of thorns for how can she be sure that the prince will not let her down? Thorn-hedges are easy to flatten; fear-of-rejection-walls are strongly built and do not yield to swords or Jericho horns. Hurt people are like the Fen villagers who 'built their homes with doors that could not be opened from the outside' (Chamberlain, 1983, p.20).

Children frightened of the dark may call for a light; frightened of rejection they may make no sound. They cannot batter at the door of a locked room; the lock is on their own feelings and the handle is on the inside. If they try to climb the wall to overcome fear, they may become paralysed or fall. Safer to stay on the ground. It is easy to mistake the disguised signs of fear for bravado, truculence, delinquency, deceit. Only by really attending to children can their cries be heard, hard to detect, but desperate, like those of babies buried under rubble.

Clarification and information

Perhaps the greatest single source of fear for children (and me) is not knowing what is going to happen. Hospital, for example, 'has a great deal of potential for inducing fear and unhappiness in its patients' (Müller, *et al.*, 1986, p.113). An important focus of work is help to face the unknown and to attain mastery. This entails clarification through helping children identify their fears and the very unknown-ness of the future, and through giving straightforward information in acceptable and comprehensible ways.

Some fears can be dispelled simply by these two expedients. In *Respecting Children* I wrote of a boy who 'read *The Hunchback of Notre Dame* and asked if *he* might grow a hump.' The question 'might have reflected a deep anxiety about physical handicap ... such questions can only be asked if some sensitive and caring adult is on hand to hear and to respond. The answer to 'Could I grow a hump?' is not 'No, of course not' (Crompton, 1980, p.122).

I now add that, early in the process of seeking for a hidden anxiety, it is kind to dispel the expressed fear, to find the right way of saying, 'No, of course not.'

Suppose that boy did have and eventually expressed a deeper fear of becoming physically handicapped, how to help him attain mastery? Most important would be to deal with him honestly. A close relation might suffer such crippling illness as arthritis. The boy himself might feel and fear distortion of his own body. He might suffer unspecific terror stimulated by *The Hunchback*.

Body images

Fear about the developing body is common at whatever age. This is an era of body-consciousness: diet, weight, smoking. Women in their 40s and 50s are faced with the problem of deciding whether or not to use hormone replacement therapy, not only to alleviate distressing symptoms and to prevent future illness, but also to retain youthful appearance and mobility. We are offered means to control the development of our bodies as never before and it is very frightening. Children and young people in adolescence have not (yet) been offered such control although doctors may prescribe contraceptive drugs to adolescent girls. Their growth and the sensations of sexual development are involuntary.

Carson McCullers captures this in her novel about a young girl, *The Member of the Wedding*. Frankie

> stood before the mirror and she was afraid. It was the summer of fear, for Frankie, and there was one fear that could be figured in arithmetic with paper and a pencil at the table. This August she was twelve and five-sixths years old. She was five feet five and three-quarter inches tall, and she wore a number seven shoe. In the past year she had grown four inches, or at least that was what she judged. ... [Already children tease her.] If she reached her height on her eighteenth birthday, she had five and one-sixth growing years ahead of her. Therefore, according to mathematics and unless she could somehow stop herself, she would grow to be over nine feet tall. And what would be a lady who is over nine feet high. She would be a Freak.
>
> (McCullers, 1962, p.25)

Frankie is helped by the straightforward response of her brother's fiancée who said 'she didn't think I looked so terribly big. She said she got the major portion of her growth before she was thirteen' (p.42).

In their survey of (approximately) four-year-old girls, Valerie Walkerdine and Helen Lucey found that all in the sample expressed fears about growing up, getting older and having to leave their mothers.

They were often found 'trying to sleep in baby cots or pushchairs, places that were far too small for them to sleep in. Often their mothers tried to resist this but the girls who used these strategies were fairly adamant. Sarah sits in the baby's buggy: Mother: That's a very silly place to lie. Child: Why? Mother: I mean it's too small. (Child climbs into the buggy anyway)' (Walkerdine and Lucey, 1989, pp.166–7). This is reminiscent of *Alice's Adventures In Wonderland* where the child becomes larger and smaller, finding magic ways to control growth.

Although such control is impossible, there is or should be a moment when we discover self, begin to know the distinction between 'me' and the rest of creation. Richard Hughes's Emily suddenly realized

> that she was *she*. She stopped dead, and began looking over all of her person which came within the range of eyes. She could not see much, except for a fore-shortened view of the front of her frock, and her hands when she lifted them for inspection: but it was enough for her to form a rough idea of the little body she suddenly realized to be hers.
>
> (Hughes, 1929, pp.134–5)

From fear to trust

Emily's self-discovery cannot save her from a nightmare of fear including capture by pirates and murder. Children in Great Britain do not usually endure such appalling experiences and they may not share Emily's intense self-discovery, but they do know about fear. They need help to identify fear, whatever its source, and to develop the sense of, and trust in, self which we all need in order to combat fear.

'Lead me from fear to trust.' We cannot lead children – hurt, betrayed, fearful – to trust unless we recognize and confront first the sources and expression of our own fears and then of the fears of the children. And that is about facing truth.

Summary

The experience of fear is universal. How we deal with it is associated with experience of, and ability to, trust, both other people and ourselves. Common foci of fear include lack of control, unknown, imagined horrors, and the repetition of known sufferings. Fear may be subdued by facing threat instead of running away, and by recognizing truth. Fear and lack of power and control may lead to withdrawal and submissiveness. Experiences of terror may be manageable if adults prove caring and trustworthy; failure of such care and trust constitute betrayal and may lead to retreat. Clear and honest information may help to reduce anxiety, for example, in relation to the fear associated with physical development and body image.

Link

To grow from fear to trust requires courage to face truth on the part of both children and adults. But what is truth? Chapter 6 offers no answers but asks some questions.

6   Speak the truth in love

What is truth?

'What is truth? said jesting Pilate; and would not stay for an answer' (Bacon, 1902, p.3). Pilate at least asked. For many people truth is either assumed or avoided. For some it is irrelevant. Even those who, like Pilate, ask the questions, like him too, many lack the will or time to seek the answer.

There is surely no answer, or no one answer. What is truth? Dictionary definitions link it with fact, which is a 'thing certainly known to have occurred or to be true' (Concise Oxford Dictionary). So I know it is a fact because it is true and it is true because it is a fact.

Many workers prepare reports for, and appear as witnesses in, courts where it is essential to distinguish between fact and opinion, 'to tell the truth, the whole truth and nothing but the truth'. Tell the truth, whole and nothing but, about everything you did yesterday. Not too difficult. What about Tuesday last week? Now try three months ago.

The whole truth

As a guardian *ad litem* (GAL) I sought to learn the truth about the lives of children who had allegedly suffered at the hands of their parents. The truth took several forms.

The legal situation had to be clear. Whatever the facts, a case could be invalidated if legislative chapter and verse were in any way inaccurate. For example, an application to a juvenile court to discharge a care order was withdrawn after discovery that the original order had not been made by that court.

The case has to be true legally in terms of being suitable to be presented to the court and once in court, proven via the machinery of evidence, witnesses, advocates, magistrates.

Everyone called to give evidence and face cross-examination, except the GAL, has direct experience of the events responsible for the application presently before the court. Social workers, health visitors, school nurses, doctors, teachers, are questioned about the aspects of the child's life with which they have been directly concerned. They can speak only about what they know to be true.

'I saw her hit him.' 'She did not bring him to the playgroup.' Provided that the witness is truthful it is possible for the truth, an objective statement of incontrovertible fact, to be told.

The mother may say, 'I didn't hit him', or 'I did take him to the playgroup', and it may be possible to prove that either the witness or the mother is not telling the truth. Is lying. Or of course is mistaken. But a mistake is not truth or fact and can have powerful effects.

Nothing but the truth

Children's futures are determined by adults with professional or personal interests telling the impossible truth. Impossible because, apart from the obvious and deliberate lies, most deviations from the truth derive surely from the difficulty of defining fact or reality. Context and expectation are so important.

As a GAL I visited everyone I could find who had any contact with and/or responsibility for the child. One worker might say 'I've never seen such dirt and untidiness. She does nothing for those children. Just sits around smoking. It's disgraceful and they should be in permanent care. No, there's no love there.'

Another might consider that 'those children are so well turned out. Clothes aren't new, she comes to our jumble sales. But she does try. They're not gleaming clean when they arrive but they're always on time and we can easily give them a scrub if the smell's a bit too high. It'd be a tragedy to keep them away from her. She meets them every afternoon and their faces light up and they run to her.'

It is hard enough to sort out from such a mixture of fact and opinion, observation and feeling, the truth about dirt and love, but worse when the opinions are about cruelty and abuse: did she, could she have burnt or bruised the child? Reliable people have been prepared to swear 'Yes' and equally reliable people 'No' to the same question about the same people and the same alleged incident. What *is* truth? And how do we know it when we see it?

This problem is beautifully illustrated in the novel *The Truth About Lorin Jones*. Researching the biography of the dead painter, Polly Alter gains from the many people who knew her different and often contradictory pictures. The search for truth is complicated by Polly's investment in the Lorin she wants to discover and a developing identification with her. Eventually she identifies

> the shy little girl Lolly Zimmern; the flaky college freshman Laurie; the young bohemian art student; the ambitious, calculating young professional ... and the neurotic, unworldly artist ... [She also finds] the poetic lost child Laura whom Garrett Jones had married, and the obsessed genius who had died in Key West. According to her niece, Lorin was generous and sensitive; her stepmother remembered her as selfish and spiteful.

Polly realizes that no one was lying, 'not wholly anyhow: everyone had told her the truth as he or she knew or imagined it' and 'most of them also had different versions of the other people in Lorin's life'. (Lurie, 1989, pp.286–7)

This can prove a serious problem for workers responsible for the care and welfare and future of children, particularly when a change of home and/or court proceedings is involved. *Mandy* (10) told GAL truthfully on one occasion that she wished to remain in care, on the next that she longed to return to her family and on the third that she feared her parents and never wanted to go to them. She told the solicitor firmly that she wanted to go home. She told no lies. She spoke on each occasion as she truly felt, then.

Un-truth

Children are told downright lies by the nicest and most honest people in order to spare them. How does it spare anything so to deprive the child of trust, in the sense of both failing to trust children and betraying their trust in adults? How can they trust people who have lied?

In *Catherine: A tragic life – The story of a young girl who died of Anorexia Nervosa*, Maureen Dunbar writes of her four-year-old daughter's stay in hospital for removal of adenoids. When the mother had to leave, the child 'clung to me sobbing and screaming. Tears were streaming down my face too – I couldn't bear to leave her. There were no facilities for mothers to stay with their children and visiting was strictly limited to set times. Eventually, I was able to leave when I assured her I would be staying upstairs in the "Mummies Ward".' Next day she 'learned from one of the other mothers that Kate had cried her heart out for me . . .' (Dunbar, 1987, pp.15, 16).

We all fail to face and tell the truth which would help children find and face the truth because we are taught to fear and avoid. Think of the euphemisms for death: passed over, gone, gone to sleep, kicked the bucket, popped his clogs. . . .

Arriving at a 'retirement home' to say goodbye to an old friend who had had a stroke we were told by the matron 'I'm afraid you may be too late.' I had sat for some minutes holding my friend's hand, wondering if I should recognize the moment of death, when my husband gently persuaded me that the matron's words had meant she was already dead.

Not long ago children placed for adoption lost for ever their birth parents. Secrecy and shame hid the real circumstances of conception. Birth and adoptive parents were kept apart. Children were supposedly replanted into new family beds to root and blossom as if sown there. Adopters were encouraged to tell children that they were adopted but many, for sure, refrained. When a woman could adopt her daughter's illegitimate child, how many grew up calling mother 'sister' and grand-mother 'mum'?

In his novel *The Skater's Waltz* Philip Norman introduces Gaye and her 'big sister' Olwen. Louis, meeting Gaye at his father's skating rink, 'thought it rather strange for Olwen to have a sister young enough to be her daughter' and considered that 'Anyone would think the girl preferred her big sister's company to that of her real Mummy and Daddy.' The mystery is never expounded but there are glimpses of Gaye's confused home life, not least olfactorily for she 'frequently wet her knickers: a fact which the adult world seemed to view with amusement', and had always about her 'the odour of wee-wee' (Norman 1979, pp.166, 177).

Telling the truth in adoption remains difficult and painful. Adopters are expected and encouraged to tell their children as much as possible as soon as possible. Birth parent/s and adopters may meet shortly before placement.

Children who know their birth parents may wish to discover them-selves changelings at least, if not actually fantasizing other and better parents. Grace in Fay Weldon's novel *Female Friends*, was

> first and only child of Edwin and Esther Songford. Or so they assumed – Grace had a tendency to deny their parentage .... [She liked] to allocate herself in her mind, throughout her childhood and afterwards, to many a rich and noble couple.
>
> (Weldon, 1975, p.21)

Philip (15), adopted by a Jewish American couple, said 'I happen to like opera a lot, so for a while my real mother was Maria Callas. She was such a strange and wonderful lady, and I thought it was neat to have such a bizarre and exotic mother' (Krementz, 1984, p.67).

Truth for adopted children may entail revelations of shock not stardom. The past may include incest, murder, neglect, abandonment. How do you speak those truths? Not at all, unless in love and with the greatest care for the welfare of the child.

Fay Weldon illustrates how not to. Stanhope, Grace's illegitimate son, has been told that his father, a (mythical) pilot, died in an air crash the day after his birth. He lives with Chloe, Grace's friend, and rarely sees his mother. Grace telephones him, a rare event.

> Grace: Stanhope darling, there's something I have to tell you. How old are you, dear?
> Stanhope: Twelve.
> Grace: Well, that's quite old enough. You know the facts of life and so on. Now listen. Are you listening?
> Stanhope: Yes.
> Grace: Your father was not that other husband of mine, the air-pilot, but a very important and talented portrait painter called Patrick Bates.

Stanhope: But that's Kev and Kes's father. Only they never see him. He's mad.

Grace: He isn't mad, he's very talented. If I were you I'd be proud of having such a famous father instead of finding fault instantly. Chloe will tell you all about it, she's good at explaining that kind of thing.

Used to an unusual home life Stanhope receives the news calmly, establishes with his foster mother Chloe that he may now be called Bob and returns to watch *Match of the Day*. Chloe muses 'If such a thing had happened to me, ... such a revelation between lunch and tea, I would have been finished for life. What saves those children? Television?'(pp.274–5, 276).

Stanhope could receive such a thunderbolt without concern because, never having been led to expect the truth from his mother, revelation of her lying was no shock. Trust could not be lost because there was none to lose. For most children trust would have been irremediably damaged. What else had been lied about? How could anything, now, be true?

What children cannot manage is the knowledge that adults are lying and making them collude in the lie, or the shock of sudden life-changing information revealing that lies have been told.

Properly attended to, the child helps the adult so that both can 'Seek ever to tell the truth in love' (Religious Society of Friends, 1960, para 320).

Summary

To tell the truth, the whole truth, and nothing but the truth is easier said than done. Truth has associations with evidence, fact, lies, opinion, perception, memory, feeling, imagination, context. Withholding or distorting truth in order to spare children suffering is likely to cause confusion and loss of trust.

Link

Only if adults and children can together develop trust and seek truth have they any chance of understanding one another, of being able truly to say 'I know what you mean', the subject of Chapter 7.

7   I know what you mean

As a social work student I visited a young mother and daughter. They lived in a scabby terraced house. *Pam* spent most of the time in bed and took some drug. *Gloria* was looked after. Just. They were in hiding from *Reg* who had beaten *Pam*. They faced eviction, living in squalor, penury and fear. I still remember three things clearly: *Pam*'s beauty, the dreadful room and myself.

I was 24, a virgin from a nice middle-class home and university. During two years work in an East End settlement I had seen a great deal but in my own life experienced little. We were, chronologically, about the same age; in real life terms *Pam* was an old woman and I a baby.

I sat beside her on the bed and she talked about her problems and I said, 'I know what you mean.' Reading my meticulous verbatim reports my supervisor gently asked, 'Do you?'

Misunderstanding may occur because one or both parties find verbal expression difficult. After release from the Red-Room Jane Eyre was interviewed by Mr Lloyd the apothecary. Jane confesses that she is 'unhappy – very unhappy,' but she cannot respond to Mr Lloyd's invitation to explain.

> How much I wished to reply fully ...! How difficult it was to frame any answer! Children can feel, but they cannot analyse their feelings; and if the analysis is partially effected in thought, they know not how to express the result of the process in words.
>
> (Brontë, 1966, p.56)

Jane can only 'frame a meagre, though, as far as it went, true response'.

Since kind Mr Lloyd has no means of knowing what Jane is not saying he bases his responses on the verbal information she offers. Humpty Dumpty is more precise.

> 'How old did you say you were?' Alice ... said 'Seven years and six months.' 'Wrong! ... You never said a word like it!' 'I thought you meant "How old *are* you?"' Alice exclaimed. 'If I'd meant that, I'd have said it,' said Humpty Dumpty.
>
> (Carroll, 1948, p.113)

Mr Lloyd responded to the answer he thought was intended. Alice answered the question she thought was meant. Neither listened to the meaning behind the words. Both thought they had understood.

Lewis Carroll plays more with the child's love of nonsense words and the adult's need to attribute meaning in *Jabberwocky*, written backwards so that it can be read only by holding the page in front of a mirror. Humpty Dumpty obligingly translates the nonsense and kills the poetry:

> ' "*the wabe*" is the grass-plot round a sundial, I suppose?' said Alice. . . .
> 'Of course it is. It's called "*wabe*", you know, because it goes a long
> way before it, and a long way behind it.' 'And a long way beyond it on
> each side,' Alice added.
>
> (pp.118–20)

This is fun, a child discovering language. But how easily Alice accepts the conversion of nonsense into meaning, quickly contributing interpretations of her own. The punning wabe explained becomes a sensible noun. Now that wabe has been defined, confined within its own description, we can all recognize one. Accepting nonsense rules and adding to the illusion of meaning is a way in which we contribute towards the limitation of our freedom.

Wabe is easy, provided that we understand grass plot and sundial. Other words are less amenable to confinement. Mr Lloyd invites Jane to discuss her future: 'Would you like to go to school?' A simple question? But Jane 'scarcely knew what school was.' Her ideas are based mainly on the highly coloured account of the maid. The disadvantages appear to be that 'young ladies sat in the stocks, wore backboards, and were expected to be exceedingly genteel and precise.'

Advantages of schooling include learning to paint, sing, play, net purses and translate French books. Jane finds her 'spirit . . . moved to emulation . . . . Besides, school would be a complete change.' She tells Mr Lloyd 'I should like to go to school.' Jane thinks she knows what Mr Lloyd means by 'school'. Mr Lloyd thinks he knows what Jane means. Both are wrong (Brontë, p.57).

Such conversations are repeated daily between kind misunderstanding adults and sad not-understanding children involved in decisions about concrete matters which they cannot possibly conceptualize in the abstract. Caring Mr Lloyd makes no attempt to discover what Jane understands by school. How could he have found out? More discussion might have involved the exchange of more words but not of meanings, because of the inability to understand the contexts in which the words were used.

Mr Lloyd is a person rare in literature and life; he did try to listen to the child, to ask questions which he thought she could understand and to attend to her answers. Although he might have discovered that Jane had based her decision to go to school on false evidence, he had gone a great deal further than most people in seeking her true wish. More

common is the behaviour which enacts 'He's too young to under-
stand/know what he wants; children are resilient (? they bounce when
you drop them); children don't know what's best for them.'

Seven-leagued boots

When Nigel Hunt (7) with Down's Syndrome entered a 'school for
backward children' his father told the head that he could read. 'He
smiled pityingly. Unbelievably, it was almost a year before he was
forced to admit that Nigel *could* read. "But of course he does not
understand what he is reading," was his face-saving comment. "Then
how do you explain the fact that we can write Nigel a note telling him
to do something and he does it? ..." The answer was a shrug of
annoyance' (Hunt, 1982, p.14).

When the beloved older brother of Maggie Tulliver (9) (*The Mill on
the Floss*) is to go away to school she asks the intermediary, Mr Riley

> 'How far is it, please, sir?' 'Oh, a long way off,' that gentleman being of
> the opinion that children, when they are not naughty, should always
> be spoken to jocosely. 'You must borrow the seven-leagued boots to
> get to him.'
>
> (Eliot, 1979, pp.20–1)

Although Mr Riley has not misunderstood Maggie, she has received
his message perfectly. 'She began to dislike Mr Riley; it was evident
that he thought her silly and of no consequence' (Eliot, 1979, pp.20–1).

Refreshingly honest is Elizabeth Taylor's description of two children
brought together to become friends. Oliver's mother offers a musical
box which Felicity's father accepts,

> in the robust tone of one who does not attempt to understand his
> children. The two children went rather desperately from the room. 'They
> are quite at our mercy,' Julia said. 'How abominable of us.' 'Children
> are better in one another's company'.
>
> (Taylor, 1988, p.108)

When the friendship, which develops happily, ends abruptly because of
his family's move, Oliver reflects that his mother 'considered, apparently, one friend as good as another for a child' (p.209).

Even when adults consider that they understand children there is no
guarantee that the young recipient of understanding feels understood.
Whenever Alice, narrator of a story by Beryl Bainbridge, has

> what they call 'problems' at school, I'm sent to the clinic to be
> understood by some psychologist with a nervous twitch, and he tells
> me it's perfectly natural to steal from the cloakroom and to cheat in

French, and anyway it's all my mother's fault. They didn't have a clinic in Mother's day, so I expect she's riddled with guilt.

(Bainbridge, 1980, p.61)

Fun in a story, but not in real life. Jo Westgate found that her child psychiatrist, 'was trying to "slot me into a pigeon-hole",' that he had a model of adolescent girls which she did not fit. Not fitting seemed to imply that she was 'odd.' For example, she did not have 'strings of boy friends', or like discos, and she did talk freely to her parents; all, apparently, highly unusual in teenage girls. She 'felt that all would have been well for Dr X is she had confessed to repressing anger or being jealous of her pregnant mother'.

Whereas Jo's ' "food problems and so on started before Mummy even conceived Thomas", she found Dr X's comments about her upbringing critical and insulting to herself and her family. And she felt that he was "rummaging around inside me to find a me I didn't want to find" – not from fear of finding an unacceptable "me" but because the psychiatrist seemed to be trying to impose characteristics which Jo did not possess' (Crompton, 1982, pp.10, 11). Through this painful time Jo achieved tremendous understanding but despite, not because of, the intervention of the caring adult.

The adult's not-understanding may derive from failure of imagination or from too great devotion to the worker's own view of the world and what is right. The gentle story of Annette (16) who becomes pregnant, Damon (15) the father, and social worker Caroline Berry is full of not-understanding. Annette wants to have the baby but her imagined future is romantic.

Because Annette is 16, has a case history and is not very bright and Damon earns £18 a week in a supermarket, the helping adults, general practitioner, consultant and social worker, assume that abortion is the right, the only course of action. Eventually Caroline Berry persuades Annette to go to the hospital.

'There'll be other babies. When you're older. When you've had time to grow up yourself and to know whether Damon is the right person to share your life with.' 'He is.' [Caroline] felt a sort of surprised respect for the girl. 'You have to be sure.' 'Can you ever be that sure?' . . . . [While Caroline is away briefly Annette leaves] 'Let her go. If they ask me to chase her up, I'll refuse. The hell with them'.

(Webster, 1980, pp.187, 188)

Through achieving some understanding of her client she also achieves crucial understanding of herself.

Listen behind the words

Sometimes responsible adults do have to override children's stated preferences. When *Mandy* continually changed her mind about whether or not she wished to return home to her family the guardian *ad litem* (GAL) and solicitor had, individually and together, to decide what recommendation to make to court. They could not simply accept her most recent swing but based their opinion on consideration of her total behaviour and communication as they understood it.

The GAL, solicitor and residential staff tried hard to listen to *Mandy*. If they had attended only to her words they would have had little chance of hearing her. They were painfully aware that whatever decision was made, it could not be right for the alternatives available offered no one right course of action, as *Mandy*'s vacillations indicated.

Mandy's behaviour and words often expressed strong and conflicting feelings. People who work with children are alert to the meaning and feelings behind the words but it is perpetually difficult to steer between unjustified and over elaborated interpretation and too superficial response. Clare Winnicott records an interview between a 12-year-old boy in residential care and a field social worker.

The boy expressed fear that his father might die; 'I hate it when he goes out on his bicycle because I always think that he will be brought home dead.' Here 'the Child Care Officer lost her nerve and said: "Well, when I saw your father last week he didn't look at all ill, in fact he was looking very well." This statement is in the language of facts, and it simply does not reach feeling, and moreover it creates a gulf between the adult and the child' (Winnicott, 1979, p.72).

She warns that 'the question of language ... means that we have to be constantly aware of which language the children are speaking in and to answer them in the same terms, otherwise we shall block communication and leave them frustrated and even more helpless than ever of being understood' (p.73). Do not answer until you can truly say message received and understood. Communicating with children can easily become a game of Chinese whispers, words without meanings, sounds without sense passed from one to another.

D. June Ellis writes from experience as a teacher and head of a Quaker boarding school of an occasion when she did not attend even to the words of one of her pupils. She reflects on 'the importance of listening not just to what people were saying but to what they were not saying, and ... to what they were really meaning.'

On one occasion, 'a youngster kept coming up to me and I answered what I thought the question was going to be; at the end of a week she stood resolutely between me and the door clutching a piece of paper asking if she could discontinue my lessons.... I had been answering unasked questions and missing the point of contact' (Ellis 1981, p.2).

A child's capacity for understanding must never be discounted. W. David Wills, head of an experimental approved school for boys in the 1960s recalled:

> some young Community Service Volunteer girls [who] had been introduced partly because of the general difficulty of finding suitable women but also because it was thought that some young attractive girls about the place would help to normalise this masculine environment. They were a resounding success, they had no preconceived ideas, no traditions, no axes to grind, they were just perfectly natural girls, and they were encouraged to be just that, though not without a good deal of encouragement when those difficulties arose ....
>
> Outstanding among them in the early days was a blind girl of 18 who with great courage and integrity, making no use whatever of her affliction to gain pity, sympathy or special treatment, received from these deprived and brutal boys not only displaced animosity, crudely expressed, but even ill-natured abuse about her blindness. Yet her persistent gentleness found its way to a corresponding quality – deeply buried, rarely expressed, self-despised – in these rough and apparently unfeeling boys.
>
> She was sitting beside one of them in the small sitting room of the Cottage one evening. He was rolling a cigarette and when she became aware of this she said something to the effect that she supposed it was a thing she couldn't do. He replied, as he usually did, with stupid but wounding abuse for a while, then paused, and said in a rough, embarrassed way, 'You can.' She, surprised, asked what he meant – how did he know what she could and couldn't do? He replied – what a world of significance was in his reply – 'I practised it in bed for two hours last night with my eyes shut.' Behind all his truculent ill-nature he had been aware of her, had put himself in her place, had, in however limited a manner, sympathized with her, had tried to find out what is was like to be blind
>
> (Wills, 1971, pp.125–6).

Properly attended to, children can help adults understand what they mean, although not all have the perseverance of June Ellis's pupil. When she really heard Annette, Caroline Berry understood both her client and herself.

A friend told me about her granddaughters *Becky* (3) and *Martha* (8). After their father had left home, *Becky* would climb into bed with her mother *Ruth*. *Becky*: 'When I'm frightened I've got *Martha* to save me. When *Martha*'s frightened she's got you to save her. You haven't got anyone to save you.' *Ruth*: 'But I'm not afraid to be alone. I like to be alone.'

Reassured, *Becky* ceased entry to her mother's bed. But *Ruth* realized that her bitterness might have been received by *Becky* as fear of loneliness so that she understood more about not only her daughter but also her own emotions and their involuntary communication. She could do this only by being courageously ready to recognize the implications of her daughter's behaviour for herself. How easy it would have been to welcome *Becky* into bed taking comfort from the little girl and encouraging dependence. Or to send *Becky* back to her own room telling her not to be silly. *Ruth*'s loving listening achieved gains for every member of the family, including her mother, my friend.

The wrong end of the stick

'In working with children,' writes Patricia Curtis, a family placement worker with National Children's Homes, 'one thing is certain: if you have the wrong end of the stick, the child will tell you' (Curtis, 1982, p.28). Annette told Caroline Berry, the pupil told June Ellis, although both had to work hard to be heard. Indeed, since actual words were ineffective both had to resort to visual rather than aural impact. Annette demonstrated her feelings by withdrawing her presence, the pupil by substituting written for verbal communication. Doubtless *Becky* would have found ways of letting her mother know if *Ruth* held the wrong end of the stick.

Working with Darren (7) who was to move into a new family Patricia Curtis watched as 'He put a figure of a happy boy into the doll's house and two angry boy figures "on top of the mountain".' She described what she had seen but, 'I had it wrong. Darren took a deep breath and said "Noooo!" Gave a sigh and, taking hold of the two angry figures said, "These aren't two angry boys any more. They are two social workers and they're in wheelchairs. I'll put them on top of the mountain because they're all muddled up"' (Curtis, 1982, p.28).

She also describes how Malcolm (7) helped residential social worker Polly to understand him. 'He often took Polly out for walks, first round the house because he was afraid to go any further, then round the block and eventually into the park across the road. He always said he was taking her to London. We didn't understand the significance of this until one day he asked "Was I borned or did I come from London?"' (p.29).

Miles Hapgood and Craig (13) were eventually able to acknowledge their difficulties in understanding each other and the benefits of their interaction: 'my own feelings towards Craig began to reflect those of his social worker and carers, which had been vividly described before I started.' The boy 'enjoyed the company and the attention', but 'saw less and less relevance in the work.' He asked Miles to 'take him swimming like all his other social workers had done. I felt strong feelings of exasperation and there were times when I could cheerfully have locked him up permanently inside some arcade machine. I had serious doubts about the realism of the family placement plan.'

Craig commented: 'I can't remember much about the early meeting. What I found most interesting was when I was doing the photography bit because then I was interested in cameras. Miles brought me an album.' He 'found out some things I didn't know before, like where I was exactly born and about my mother, but I don't think it made much difference. I did not find a flow chart thing very interesting. It wasn't my way of putting things down because I was very into games. That's all I could think about then' (Hapgood, 1988, p.93–4).

Miles Hapgood and Craig could recognize and express the discrepancies in their views of their shared interaction. A study of the experiences of children, parents and social workers in the many aspects of care demonstrated that the perceptions and responses of each participant in any one event might be diverse and often unreconciled. At all points decisions might be taken by social workers with minimal if any consultation and both parents and children would be left for ever bewildered (Fisher *et al.*, 1986).

Summary

It is often tempting to assume understanding of another person because a common language is spoken. Adults may fail to understand children because of inappropriate assumptions that they lack ability, intelligence and awareness. Responses may be, for example, patronizing, or dismissive, in accordance with false expectations of children's real messages. Even when it is necessary to override children's expressed wishes, it is essential to listen behind the words. Properly attended to, children help adults understand what they really mean, and to recognize when they have misunderstood.

Link

In order accurately to attribute meaning to words and behaviour, it is necessary really to attend to both the other person and oneself, to look and listen and feel, to 'Be here now', the subject of Chapter 8.

8 Be here now

Be here now

Miles Hapgood, evaluating his work with Craig (13), writes 'we were struck by how our enthusiasm for applying new techniques took us away from some basic social work principles', including 'starting where the client is' (Hapgood, 1988, p.100). It is hard enough to identify one's own state of being and here and now, let alone discovering and then relating to and communicating with that of another person, any other person and particularly one who is not very articulate and is in apparent need of help.

Unless the worker does start where the client is, no progress is possible. The very intention to start there is in itself progress. The intention really to attend to the client is in itself the communication of attention.

Workers seem still to be surprised that children need and demand attention. Sarah Mumford, new to working with children, well supervised and very honest, experienced difficulty in making contact with James until 'we went out together and bought some hamburgers,' which he would eat only 'in the children's home where he clearly enjoyed the attention of Sarah and two female members of staff. The description of James sitting on the adults' knees in turn, drinking from each of their coffee cups, revealed the toddler that was struggling to get out of this now 14-year-old body.'This led to understanding of his 'basic need for attention and comfort' and the development of 'an appropriate programme for him'.

Sarah Mumford was evidently helped by the ability of her supervisor to be with her, to start where she was. Then she could find out where James was. 'The first work focused on the senses, and involved games based on taste, smell, touch, sound and sight', on reality, on the sense of self, of being. 'James began to enjoy his sessions thoroughly and they became very important to him.'

The ability really to be with the child demands the ability to be aware of oneself. Sarah Mumford's difficulties with Lennox were resolved only when she and Eva Banks 'were able to recognize that Sarah was fearful about failing with him' (Banks and Mumford, 1988, pp.107, 108, 109).

Working with teenage Sasha and Jan, Dominic Dubois felt 'frightened at times about telling . . . the truth around their mother's desertion.' He found compiling a chronological history 'most painful' but gained 'the capacity . . . to subsequently share the pain in their lives. . . . It is no coincidence that I was only able to finish this work after doing a flow chart of my own life' (Adcock, Dubois and Small, 1988, p.127).

Miles Hapgood, having 'reached a staged of impasse, with all the attendant feelings of disappointment and frustration on my part,' with Craig, realized that 'Insufficient thought had been given to adapting the direct work techniques to Craig's particular strengths and weaknesses. Rather than consider his overriding interest – arcade games – and examine how this could be harnessed, we had regarded this interest as an obstacle to the real job at hand.'

Once he made this step towards the real Craig he learnt that 'our attitude . . . mirrored Craig's own attitude to previous life experiences – ignore it and it might all go away' (p.94).

Janet Galley recognized that her own view of Joyce's future welfare interfered with her ability to attend to the girl herself. 'I thought about my own role and decided I was probably adding to her confusion . . . because I had already committed myself to the idea of adoption, I could not really take on board the idea of Deed Poll. I thought Joyce was picking up my feelings about this' (Aldgate and Galley, 1988, p.69).

In order to be able to make these comments Janet Galley needed to be in honest touch with not only her own feelings but also Joyce's response to them. She had to listen behind words, to listen and not just to hear.

In *Zen Practice in Social Work*, David Brandon describes becoming 'physically centred in an interview; I focus on the sound of the words spoken by the client so that my personal internal noises are moderated and can hear. I try to respond both to the questioner and the question in an unhurried way, picking out the colour and content of the communication.'

He had once 'videotaped an interview with a client . . . an uncomfortable experience. I felt that the client was very angry, almost bullying and curt in response to my questions. When I played back the recording my own fear was much more obvious than his aggression' (Brandon, 1979, p.34).

Looking and seeing

American artist Ernest W. Watson wrote about looking and seeing. 'Looking is but a superficial experience which does not promote intimate acquaintance, does not go to the heart of things. . . . We may be made aware of this gap between looking and seeing if asked . . . to describe the furnishings of a room in which we have been visiting.' (Watson, 1985, p.31).

A residential social worker realized during a training session that she did not know what one of the girls in her care had been wearing that morning, skirt or jeans; she had seen her but not *seen* her.

Ernest W. Watson continues 'We see, *really see*, when we lose self-consciousness in contemplation of scenes, objects, or events. Only then can we be said to integrate with the subject, become a part of it as happens when we witness an absorbing drama or watch a major league game. When we really see, we transcend our own individuality, forget self, and become engrossed in a visual adventure.'

He illustrates this literally with the reproduction of a drawing and verbally with the background to its creation: 'my gaze fell upon some magenta tulips. I had never before *seen* a tulip. Oh, I had looked at tulips in a long succession of springtimes and had gloried in their beauty when their colors blazoned like the gamut of color on an artist's palette. ... I had looked at innumerable tulips in a detached and agreeable kind of way for as long as I could remember; yet, until this occasion, I had never really *seen* one' (p.31).

Really seeing children has little to do with case conferences and assessment-forms, and everything to do with becoming integrated with the subject when we forget self.

The subject may be the whole of life, our own and those for whom we are responsible, in minute detail. Here is a story from the discipline of Zen:

Every-Minute Zen

Zen students are with their masters at least ten years before they presume to teach others. Nan-in was visited by Tenno, who, having passed his apprenticeship, had become a teacher. The day happened to be rainy, so Tenno wore wooden clogs and carried an umbrella. After greeting him Nan-in remarked: 'I suppose you left your wooden clogs in the vestibule. I want to know if your umbrella is on the right or left side of the clogs.'

Tenno, confused, had no instant answer. He realized that he was unable to carry his Zen every minute. He became Nan-in's pupil, and he studied six more years to accomplish his every-minute Zen

(Reps, 1971, p.43).

Such awareness of oneself or of another person is felt and communicated in ways outside our ordinary sense of time and space. Philippa Pearce writes about Kate (10) who needs with increasing desperation to talk to her mother. Mrs Tranter fails really to attend to her daughter and so does not perceive let alone understand this need.

Eventually ignoring Kate's appeal she

turned on her heel to march out of the bedroom. Such a departure takes only a few short seconds; but Kate had time to feel a long despair. She felt it here and now; and it seemed always to have been lying in wait for

for her; and she saw it ahead of her, stretching before her like a long, long road, like the rest of her life .... [She weeps soundlessly]. In the very doorway of the bedroom, Mrs Tranter paused – she could not have said why. She listened to the silence behind her, and was disturbed by it. She turned her head, looked back over her shoulder at Kate. She saw Kate sitting up in bed, with despairing eyes from which the tears streamed without ceasing.

(Pearce, 1985, pp.81, 82)

By at last really being with her daughter Mrs Tranter is able to ask the crucial question, 'Katy, what is it?' and begin to listen to the answer.

The mouse cage

Really to attend to a troubled child imposes at least a demand and probably a strain which may be unwelcome if not intolerable. Retired teacher Dennis Mitchell recalled experience as a volunteer 'in a lonely camp in the country near London' with lads who 'had committed just about every crime in the juvenile calendar from petty theft to attempted murder.' One boy approached him 'in a moment of deep confidence.'

'"You know I'm keeping mice and I'm making a cage. Come along and see it". Some sort of caution in me put him off and I said I would try to make it when I had the time.' Eventually Dennis Mitchell 'was waylaid.... First he showed me the mice, in a box as their new home was not yet finished. Then in a moment of great appeal he turned his face to mine and said, "This is my mouse cage." He waited looking as it were right inside me and trying to read the verdict in my face. I was shocked.'

The mouse cage was a shambles. 'He had taken a piece of wood to form the floor and was knocking into this long nails to form bars. These nails were the verdict on his life. Not a single one was straight. Nails knocked to one side, nails bent partly over. Twisted and tilted at every angle.'

The boy tried in increasing desperation and anger to knock the nails straight. 'Then in one astonishing moment he turned to me with outstretched arms, the hammer in one hand and the nail in the other, in a gesture of appeal. Tears streamed down the face of this young tough as he stood there, white faced, beaten, emotionally battered. "Please knock it in for me." His outstretched hands offered the hammer and the nail.' Dennis Mitchell accepted the tools and "With all the concentration I could command I knocked the nail in straight and true. Peace came over the lad. He stood utterly quiet and relaxed with even a look of gratitude' (Mitchell, 1986, pp.7–8).

Here are several examples of really being here and now. The boy was totally involved in and with his mouse cage as surely as Edgar Watson was involved in and with his tulip. For the boy the mouse cage might be the first creation he had ever attempted on his own initiative, and on his own. It was something to show, to share, and to invite attention.

Eventually it was a means of asking openly, painfully and in humiliating circumstances for help. His whole self, his deprived and delinquent history, his difficult present, his fear of the future, his sense of being a poor and failing self, all were concentrated in his concentration on the construction.

There is desperate irony in the failure of a boy likely to spend some of his life behind bars to make even an animal cage. And there is a deep sadness in his need to imprison small animals in order to control some other creature.

Such was his need and such his concentration that from the fruitless anger of his attacks on the nails he gained peace and became quiet and relaxed as soon as the young man had knocked that nail in straight.

What reached him? Relief that the job could be completed even if not by himself? Relief that he could be heard, that 'Please knock it in for me' was not ignored or rebuffed but led to exactly the response he sought, that the helper would really be with him in his own idea of his own need. I am reminded of Miles Hapgood's honesty, recognizing that in enthusiasm for techniques and agendas he had omitted to attend properly to the interests and plans of Craig himself.

Dennis Mitchell did not try to discuss the boy's wish to make a mouse cage or give a carpentry lesson, he did not suggest an alternative occupation or use the opportunity to ask why the boy had committed offences. He simply did as he was asked. Perhaps he was the first person ever to do such a thing for this boy.

But he could make the right response only when he stopped trying to avoid the boy: even then he had to be waylaid and applied all the concentration he could command, concentration on both the nail and the present situation, that is to say the presence of himself and the needy boy together and the boy's expressed need for help. He did not pause to think what would be the correct response. Because he had stopped avoiding the boy, both physically and emotionally, he could really see and hear the boy and be with him.

The cost of healing

The impact of a close encounter with a troubled child can be very disturbing and it is no surprise if adults are reluctant to risk too much. Professor of child psychiatry Michael Rutter writes of the split-second encounter between a child psychiatrist and 'a particularly difficult adolescent in the in-patient unit he ran. The boy had the habit of spitting directly in the faces of staff.... A variety of methods of response were tried without effect; the spitting got worse, the staff were in a state of continual tension, and most felt a humiliating mixture of anger and despair in their not knowing what to do.'

During a long staff meeting it was decided, with misgivings, 'to break the unit's long-standing prohibition against the use of corporal punishment by staff ... the very next time the boy spat in the face of anyone, that person should immediately hit the boy in the face.' On leaving the meeting the psychiatrist was 'greeted by the offending child with the usual spit in the face. As agreed, he hit the boy. The result was dramatic. The boy was obviously both astonished and deeply upset by this unexpected violence from a gentle, loving man – he never ever spat again.' The man, too, was deeply affected; 'he was so disturbed by his own feelings in giving way to violence and to the recognition that part of him *wanted* to hit back in anger, that he realized that he could never ever do that again' (Rutter, 1983, pp.90–1).

The boy was helped but at considerable cost to the adult, although his increased self-awareness may have been a gain. A real encounter leads to change in all concerned.

This experience must have been exhausting. You cannot give so much of yourself, even in a split second, without giving energy. Workers in all fields often offer as a reason for not engaging in direct work with children that they have too little time. Energy is often in even shorter supply than time, partly because so much is drained off in anxiety (too little support and too much demand) and misplaced priorities (administration, meetings, complicated systems).

In order to make real contact with a child you may need very little time but a great deal of will. Even a short real contact costs energy if help and healing are to result. Here is a story about a great healer and lover of children:

> As he went, the people pressed round him. And a woman, who had had
> a flow of blood for twelve years and could not be healed by any one,
> came up behind him, and touched the fringe of his garment; and
> immediately her flow of blood ceased. And Jesus said, 'Who was it that
> touched me?' When all denied it, Peter said, 'Master, the multitudes
> surround you and press upon you!' But Jesus said, 'Someone touched
> me; for I perceive that power has gone forth from me.'
>
> (Luke 8:40–46, Revised standard version, 1952).

Jesus was on his way to the dying 12-year-old daughter of Jairus. But he was not racing around anxious and excited by the emergency. He might be expected to need all his energy for the task ahead but he did not reprimand the woman for taking power from him. He was surrounded by people and might be expected not to notice one touch more than another.

But he was so present, so here, that he knew, and gave not only the power, the healing, through involuntary physical contact, but also the kindness of reassurance through deliberate recognition. The woman who had hidden herself in the crowd and been afraid openly to ask for help, realized that she had been noticed and 'came trembling, and falling down before him declared in the presence of all the people why she had touched him, and how she had been immediately healed. And he said to her, "Daughter, your faith has made you well; go in peace."' (Luke 8:47–48).

Not 'sorry love, you've got your cure, now I really must press on,' but 'go in peace.'

He was really present with the daughter of Jairus too, for a while everyone else was busy weeping and bewailing, he looked at, really saw the real child and could say 'she is not dead but sleeping.' He touched her and then, always fully conscious of the needs of the whole real present person, 'he directed that something should be given her to eat.' (Luke 8:52–56).

Making notes after a training session at a community home, where staff were very tired, I wrote 'power has gone forth from me.' Residential staff are surely in this position all the time whether being physically touched or drawn on emotionally and psychically (if there is a differ- ence!) They are involved in healing *all* the time, whether or not in a/the special room and will be taken-from in ways of which they are unconscious. Power goes forth all the time merely by exposure to the children (and to colleagues who also have needs and make demands).

During the first half of the session staff had been very sluggish and I had felt anxious at the lead-balloon response to what I had hoped would be interesting and stimulating material. Power was oozing out of me fast. Someone commented, 'I hadn't realized we were all so tired.' Power had gone forth and gone forth and gone forth.

Pearl saw *May* for an hour a week, trying to help her gain some sense of self and find, first her present and eventually her past. There were fears that she was in danger of becoming 'frozen' and losing touch with reality and emotion. She found *May* responsive and enjoyed the sessions but was amazed to discover herself to be very tired at the end and realized that she had been concentrating entirely on *May*, attending to her closely and that power had passed from her, particularly at a time of crisis.

Thinking about Luke's narration I failed to wonder why Jesus forced the woman to declare herself. He could have noticed but not remarked on the sense that he had been taken-from. G. B. Caird suggests that if the woman 'had been allowed to slip away in a comfortable obscurity, one of two things would have happened: either she would have suffered a relapse, brought on by a sense of guilt at having broken the laws of uncleanness; or she would have enjoyed a permanent cure, but without seeing in it the gateway to a richer and more abundant life ...' (Caird, 1963, p.124).

Recognition by the healer of the patient includes emotional, spiritual and social needs. Under Jewish law the menstruating woman is unclean and should on no account have touched the man. In order really to be clean and thus healed from social stigma, it was important that she was publicly declared so. She could no longer be defined, as are so many people in our own society, as a non-person because of some disability or disadvantage. And she needed to accept herself as whole and healed in order to avoid relapse.

In contrast to the publicity following the healing of this woman, Jesus instructed the parents of the girl whom he soon gently revived 'to tell no one what had happened,' another instance of really being with the needy person. Jesus understood that a convalescent child would need peace and her parents. She would certainly not need crowds of sensation-seekers gawping at her. Her parents too needed a quiet time with her. The fuss (probably substantially the work of professional mourners) following her supposed death had created quite enough disturbance.

In his work with Craig, Miles Hapgood recognized the importance of suiting the technique to the need of the individual child. The treatment by Jesus of the woman and the girl offers excellent models.

There are many kinds of death. Work with children is often concerned with reviving dead or frozen emotions, in calling back the fleeing spirit, in helping the lost child to be here now.

Summary

Effective communication can be achieved only when adults really attend to children, which includes recognizing such feelings as fear of failure and frustration. Only really looking, listening and feeling can lead to understanding. Real communication may be very costly to the caring adult in terms of energy, self-knowledge and emotion. But paying the price may help a child to live.

Link

Part 3 has explored some of the fundamental aspects of working with children: philosophical, ethical, emotional and spiritual. Part 4 introduces a number of ideas about and illustrations of ways of communicating with children. Chapter 9 focuses on 'Talking without words'.

Part 4

9 Talking without words

Patting our curls

We rely heavily on spoken language as the chief means of communication but even when speech is available to all parties, messages are constantly given and received in other ways. The difficulty many people experience with telephone transactions illustrates the reduction of efficient communication when only one sense can be engaged. A moment's silence elicits cries of 'Are you there?'

Given a full range of senses we respond to a wide range of clues. George Eliot describes the impact of his schoolmaster's wife and 'house-mother' on the sensitive physically disabled boy Philip who

> met her advances towards a good understanding very much as a caressed
> mollusc meets an invitation to show himself out of his shell .... [She]
> was not a loving, tender-hearted woman; she was a woman whose skirt
> sat well, who adjusted her waist and patted her curls with a preoccupied
> air when she inquired after your welfare. These things doubtless
> represent a great social power, but it is not the power of love – and no
> other power could win Philip from his personal reserve.
>
> (Eliot, 1979, p.175)

Even the most loving and tender-hearted among us have patted our curls when enquiring after someone's welfare and doubtless most of us are familiar with the emotions of the caressed mollusc offered the stone of social power instead of the bread of love.

Clues given by body posture, facial expression and movement may be far more expressive than words but may easily be overlooked, for example, in the behaviour of very young children. Social worker *Jane Fisk* took a new colleague to visit 21-month-old *Len* about whom she felt anxious without being able to identify the cause. *Len* took his coat to the new worker indicating that he wanted to put it on. *Jane* saw this as a plea to a potentially new source of help, 'please take me with you', a message he had been unable to communicate to Jane herself.

A two-year-old would become rigid on the way home from nursery to his quarrelling parents. *Jane* realized that he was frightened of his father. A nine-month-old displayed terror of her mentally disturbed mother.

We are accustomed to supporting visual and behavioural clues orally. Much of the Cleveland dispute raged around the evidential sufficiency of anal dilation, essentially visual. Was oral disclosure essential? Did oral refutation or recantation override involuntary physical evidence? In her discussion of Cleveland, Beatrix Cambell writes of a boy (11), alleged to have been sexually assaulted. During the investigation of these allegations his father 'had apparently given permission for the police to push the boy as far as they felt was necessary.' Sue Richardson of the Social Services Department said 'The boy was treated like a criminal, as a perpetrator . . . .' The detective 'told us how he'd told the boy that he was a little so-and-so, that he'd push him until he cracked' (Campbell, 1988, p.75).

Waiting

Among the many lessons to be learnt from the suffering in Cleveland is the crucial importance of attending to all signs and clues and seeking balance. If oral corroboration is needed the caring worker trusts in her own observation and in the child. Moira Woods followed visual and tactile examination with gentle attention to the whole child. A little girl 'bounced in and said, "My dad hurt my bummy and made it bleed." Straight out. Her eight-year-old sister just sat; no, she said, "Everything at home is lovely." . . . I examined her – I could put two fingers in her vagina and her rectum dilated up to an inch. I said maybe there was something she forgot to tell me. She said, "Yep." After 18 months patient waiting, "She cried and cried. She only agreed to say who'd hurt her if she wrote it on a piece of paper and if I promised to tear it up. It said "Daddy". I tore it up. She had her head on my lap, and cried and cried. Don't assume for one minute that the children have told you everything. They always keep back the worst things' (Campbell, 1988, pp.32–3).

Waiting, giving time and protection from pressure to rush or push, may be a powerful form of communication to the troubled child. Marietta Higgs, as a doctor in Gateshead, worked with a girl (9) who 'had been abused by her stepfather and teenage brother'. Dr Higgs and the child 'met fortnightly for a year, with the child sitting on a rafter over a window in the Victorian clinic'. She said 'I do not think I ever, even in that length of time, managed to begin to form a relationship with this child. . . . It was a very sobering experience for me to have met that child.'

It appears to have been nearly impossible to understand the girl's behaviour. Why did she attend the clinic at all? Why did she perch on the rafter? The only verbal clue came after a year when, throughout the whole session, the girl was 'asking who would care, what would happen if she threw herself from the window. . . .' (p.40).

What do you really mean?

Meeting children in need is always a sobering experience and trying to interpret their signals cannot be undertaken lightly. Simon Wilkinson, writing on making contact with very young children, comments on interpreting 'the angle at which the head is held. . . .' He warns that 'if the previous meaning ascribed by prior care takers has been out with cultural norms, our own interpretations of the associated emotions may well be misplaced and unhelpful; for example, the apparently dejected posture may have been used to irritate prior care givers, and hence have developed alternative meanings' (Wilkinson, 1987, p.58).

Dave J. Müller *et al.* recognize that 'Children, like adults, do not always show their emotions. They may seem quiet and accepting, but deep down they may be very frightened. It is not wise to assume that a child is fine just because there is no obvious sign of distress' (Müller *et al.*, 1986, p.107). It is never safe to accept the obvious. What you see may not mean what you expect.

Alfred Torrie writing on bereaved children advises that the young child has not 'mastered the art of communication and it is rare for him to be able to say what he feels. Silent, or preoccupied with material things, adults often say "he isn't grieving! He doesn't seem to care." It is even more puzzling to relatives when an able child falls dramatically in school performance, behaves wildly or retreats into a strange silence' (Torrie, 1978, p.5).

Moreover, what you see may not be what you want. A worker may have investment in a child expressing the 'right' emotion. A busy nurse may want to believe that a child's smile indicates comfort but it may cover fear or despair. A social worker may look for distress following a disrupted foster placement when the child truly feels relief. A policeman may seek evidence to corroborate what he hopes to be true.

The Cleveland Enquiry heard that a police officer 'had responded to children's silences by reporting: "You know I've been talking to a child who is really well aware of what we're talking about, and he's emphatic nobody's touched him"' (Campbell, 1988, p.75). Since the boy was silent, what signs had he employed to indicate emphatically that no one had touched him? Did he nod in answer to straight questions or smile or frown or cry? How did the police officer know what the boy intended to convey?

The most generous interpretation is that he believed the boy intended to communicate that no one had touched him. But even well-intentioned misunderstandings can have harmful effects. Child psychiatrist Stephen Wolkind records how benign interpretation and treatment of unacceptable behaviour led to increased difficulties for child and family. Alice (12) had been successfully placed for six years following severe abuse. However, she was continually 'stealing money from her parents and two brothers. This was treated with great sympathy and under-standing but ... it emerged how very angry her parents felt about the stealing. Had it been either of their biological sons who had done this, the result would have been a good hiding. The boys too were able to say how angry Alice made them.' However, Alice could 'be treated in exactly the same way as one of her siblings. She seemed extremely relieved when she was given an angry smack on her bottom and was sent to bed by her mother for taking a five pound note. The stealing rapidly stopped' (Wolkind, 1988, pp.100–1).

Leaving aside discussion of corporal punishment, the issue here was about assumptions and interpretations. Alice's talking-without-words could be understood only by a listener prepared to attend to the whole child, indeed to the whole family, for her brothers had strong needs too.

A two-way affair

Whatever the setting and context of contact, whatever the age and ability of the child, communication can be established if the caring adult has the will. W. W. Smith in *Teaching a Down's Syndrome Child* advises, 'Attempt to establish some form of basic communication with the baby as early as possible. Communication becomes true communication only when there is feedback, i.e. a two-way affair, with one responding to the stimulus of the other' (quoted in Shaw-Champion, n.d., p.1).

The adult is expected to respond to stimulus given by the child, and not an active verbal child but a pre-vebal baby with a mental handicap. Geoff Shaw-Champion and his wife learnt to give and respond to delicate stimuli with their Down's Syndrome baby daughter Chloe, with whom they learnt the Makaton system of signing; 'we had to remember to make sure Chloe was looking at us before we gave the sign. She did seem to pick up the significance of what we were doing. We could see this occasionally in a subtle shift of her attention. Later on we were rewarded by broad grins. But in the early stages just a fleeting glance was often sufficient for her' (p.2).

Overlooked, literally, the fleeting glance may never ripen into a smile. It may be easier, less painful or demanding for adults to believe that children cannot respond at all because they do not understand.

Secure in warmth

Chloe's efforts were always rewarded 'with a cuddle or smile' (p.4). Dave J. Müller *et al.* encourage paediatric nurses to help children with 'a reassuring cuddle ... even when not requested' (Müller *et al.*, p.107).

June Jolly recognizes that 'As children get older they sometimes feel they shouldn't cry and try terribly hard not to.' It is important 'to show it does not matter if they do cry and you will understand. Gently talking about Mummy, home, admitting you know how he would like to be with them, can be comforting, if at the same time you are cuddling and perhaps gently rocking him ....' Nurses may find it 'easier and less traumatic ... to cheer him up, but it may drive the pain and anguish of the child inwards' (Jolly, 1986, p.91).

Crying itself is a form of communication inviting much attention. Parents recognize the various cries of their own babies: hunger, fear, anger, discomfort. But older children can and should cry too.

May, who had every reason to howl, did not cry even when physically hurt, but met every buffet and graze with a smile to delight a Victorian schoolmaster but not her foster mother or social worker. Joy was great on the day she came home from school with a tale of being hit on the ear by a boy. She had cried. She had screamed. She had told the teacher. The event was celebrated in her life-story book including pictures of two faces with swollen red ears, one crying, one screaming. *May* was learning, not to be a coward, but safely to stop perpetually smiling and to express a range of emotion. While the story was being told and pictures drawn *May* was being cuddled.

The girl who after 18 months told Moira Woods of her father's assault 'cried and cried ... she had her head on my lap, and cried and cried' (Campbell, 1988, p.33). The doctor no doubt needed the physical contact as much as the child. To offer comfort is often also to receive. Surely too the tears of the child were not the only ones to be shed. Caring adults must weep too.

Rachel West showed me the beautifully equipped bedroom in the maternity unit in which parents may share the last hours with their dying babies. When there is no hope of life the baby is removed from the ventilator and may be cuddled until death and as long after as the parents wish.

The connection between healthy grieving and physical comforting is made by Elizabeth Taylor:

> 'It isn't that Liz was particularly happy as a child, but she was allowed to be loving ... her mother, whom she adored, died when she was twelve. She was overwhelmed by grief, but not distracted by it. [Liz's] mother had taught her to be loving, had kissed her and tucked her in for the night, leaving her secure in warmth. She left her like that when she died. I think children must be encouraged to love or they will close up. Or hate.'
> 'Or love themselves too much'.
>
> (Taylor 1967, p.67)

To be left secure in warmth is a condition most of us seek and not only in situations of fear and loss and grief. Anger may be best met with physical comfort. Eve Hopkirk records a social worker who 'spoke of an experience with a very angry child following a review when the boy had rushed out of the room ....' He 'had followed him and held him tight, not allowing him to damage himself' and 'had held this very distressed boy until his anger gradually died away. The message conveyed to the boy not only verbally but by his actions was of acceptance and concern for his safety. He also helped him to manage the emotion, and comforted him with his physical presence' (Hopkirk, 1988, p.120).

A message of acceptance and concern for their safety was conveyed to Jerome, Cheryl and Mark by their foster parents Lily and Albert Foreman. During their three year stay 'Our task was to give them the love and attention they needed but also to let them know they would not be with us for ever.' They were in care 'because their mother could not cope with three young children. She was always leaving them at the nursery and Jerome had been in hospital several times with bruises.'

Contact with their mother resulted in much distress: 'Mark would cry bitterly and wet himself, Cheryl would stand and wet all over the floor and Jerome would roar like a wild animal, crawling around the floor and he would bite you if you got too near. We just cuddled them, held them tightly to us and let them know why they were angry and that we loved them.'

Eventually contact with the mother was stopped. 'The last time the children saw their mother she had a new baby with her. On their return of course they wanted to know why mummy had the baby and not them. We explained she could look after one child but not three. Mark said he was my baby and I cuddled him up in my arms.'

When a new social worker told the children that 'she was trying to find a new mummy and daddy for them' they became 'angry and hurt each other. After cuddles and talking to them for a long time they were calm again' (1985, p.54).

Cuddles and talking do not solve problems but they greatly strengthen the hurt or angry or frightened child and the caring adults. Children and young people can equally give comfort and strength to one another. Jean Ure has written a novel about David, a golden boy dying of cancer. He is helped to face crippled life and eventually death by Robyn (17) who held his hand and

> taught him how to dance. I didn't do it terribly well – I'm not really sure that David was any more proficient when we'd finished than when we'd started – but at the end he kissed me and said, 'Robyn, you're a catharsis!'
>
> (Ure, 1987, p.175)

Friendship grew between *Sukie* (13) in hospital with arthritis and *Rina* (12) recovering from a terrible car accident in which a parent was killed. *Rachel West* described them as 'inseparable' and the friendship as 'a godsend. They sleep close together with their arms round each other.' She foresaw 'a problem if *Sukie* goes home first.' The comfort given by *Sukie* was of a kind and quality not possible from even the most caring member of staff.

For many adults touching and cuddling a child is second nature. After reunion with her grandmother whom she had not seen for several months, *May* told *Pearl* 'Granny said "I missed you" and she cuddled me.' *Pearl* thought this showed considerable progress in *May*'s journey towards feeling and expressing a range of emotions since she narrated with great verve and illustrated it by flinging her arms around herself.

However, it is never safe to assume that a child will welcome cuddling. *Iris* (3) was desperately unhappy when placed in a foster home. *Jean*, her foster mother, experienced great distress because *Iris* would not allow her near: 'It was horrible.' After a few hours *Iris* herself approached *Jean*, who had sensitively waited for the child, not imposing physical contact out of her own need to feel that she was doing something.

Furry animals and dead budgerigars

Children who cannot tolerate physical contact with an adult may find comfort from animals. *The Trouble with Donovan Croft* tells the (fictional) story of a boy who is boarded out following his mother's desertion. Shock and fear render him mute and when he is taunted at school as 'a stupid black idiot' by his teacher, Donovan runs away. He comes to rest in the foster home's shed nursing a guinea-pig.

> Warm and trusting out of its hutch, Fluff needed him as he needed it. [He] cradled the small guinea-pig closer, still rocking to and fro, and now flattening the whirling fur with his tears. He still couldn't understand. How could his father have sent him away?
>
> [Donovan's] trust in other people was totally destroyed. He no longer wanted to have anything to do with anyone any more. He no longer wanted to go on living. [The foster father] spoke softly to Donovan, but he was not heard, for Donovan's head was filled with the mighty sound of his own miserable cry, and there was room for nothing else. 'Why, Mam, ... why?'
>
> (Ashley, 1974, p.71)

Laura Bridge takes children for walks with her dog to aid the difficult process of making speedy contact and learning about their views and wishes: 'if they don't tell me they might tell the dog.'

Superbun began a new mission as a life-saver in a paediatric ward when a magician produced him, like all magic rabbits, out of a hat. His previous career had been in a school where he was, according to *Rachel West*, 'a little bit frivolous'. *Beth*, suffering from leukaemia, was upset and anxious. *Rachel* placed *Superbun* on her lap and immediately there was something for her to cuddle and clutch on to. *Superbun* took it very well except for weeing all over her. *Lloyd* had both eyes covered after surgery and was, like *Beth*, anxious and upset. He stroked *Superbun* until he fell asleep.

The policy in *Rachel*'s ward is to allow visits from favourite pets but Jean Ure's novel includes a reminder that visiting pets may not be universally welcome. Robyn smuggles fox terrier Max into the ward where David lies gravely ill. The reunion is rapturous until Sister strikes.

> 'How *dare* you bring that animal into the wards? And to put him on a patient's *bed*! Don't you know this boy has had a leg amputated? . . . Do you realize the *germs* you have spread? . . . ' The worst part was *dis*-uniting them. I felt dreadful, prising Max away. He clung, with his front paws, and David had tears streaming down his face . . .
>
> (Ure, 1987, p.107).

The price of communication is eternal vigilance. For David the breaking of defences and the stimulus to weep, to express his terrible fear and grief might have been wonderfully helpful and healing.

Betsy Byars is more hopeful in *The Pinballs*; three foster children are

> just like pinballs. Somebody put in a dime and punched a button and out we came, ready or not, and settled in to the same groove . . . you don't see pinballs helping each other, do you? . . . soon as they get settled, somebody comes along and puts in another dime and off they go again.
>
> (Byars, 1977, p.26)

But when Harvey, whose father had accidentally driven over his legs, is in hospital, Carlie and Thomas J. smuggle in a puppy as a birthday present.

> The puppy was wriggling against Harvey's neck, and suddenly Harvey started to cry. It was the first time he had cried since the accident. It was like the turning on of a tap. He sobbed, and the tears rolled down his cheeks in streams. The puppy, wild with all the excitement, licked at the tears.
>
> (p.100)

The nurse here turns an approving blind eye.

Alfred Torrie illustrates the importance of the death of animals, not only because of the loss of the actual pet, but also the ways in which adults deal with the death and the child and the crucial often unconscious messages transmitted. He introduces the 'boy whose mother took his greatly loved cat to be "put down" without telling him. Thinking to save him (or herself) distress, she created a deep sense of insecurity and a lack of trust in herself' (Torrie, 1978, p.11).

Another mother, 'who threw the dead budgie into the dustbin in view of the child was less wise than the one who provided material for a burial' (p.7). And a 'little girl finding her pet budgie in its cage stood without a word holding it in her hand with great tears rolling down her cheeks. She was comforted by a 'proper funeral'' under the magnolia but the new budgie never replaced the first' (p.10).

How did you know that?

Honesty is the best and only policy. 'I remember one morning in the plastic surgery department where "Fred the Goldfish" had died during the night. As he was a great favourite I disposed of him quietly and told the children he was tired and he had gone to Jesus. Oh no, said a little voice, I saw you put him down the sluice this morning. Get out of that one, I thought' (Marshall, p.2).

Children receive messages through all their senses. As June Jolly says, they 'see a great deal more than adults suppose. It can never be assumed that they have not heard and seen everything that is going on in the ward. . . .' For 'the conclusions they come to . . . may be very different from the way adults view them.' She cites the example of Jackie (4) with a permanent tracheotomy who 'greeted me when I came on duty one morning with "Sister, did you know a baby died in there last night?" pointing to the bathroom. "Yes" . . . "Did they kill it in there?" . . . "No one killed the baby . . . [He] died because he wasn't strong enough to breathe anymore."' 'June Jolly had been assured "that everyone had been asleep, but had I been too quick with my answer we might not have known Jackie really thought the baby had been killed. What might the implications of that sort of memory be?"' (1981, p.92).

It is easy to overlook the capacity of children to receive and respond to the complex texture of communication with which we are all surrounded, like fish in constantly changing patterns of waves and weed, sunlight and stone. We may easily ignore the impact of the texture on people who are unconscious.

Rachel West spoke of *Rupert*, deeply unconscious in intensive care. After careful preparation by *Anna Hughes* his brother was allowed to visit. *Ralph* jumped onto the bed and put his arms round *Rupert* as if he were awake. *Rachel* and *Anna* are sure that this contact had a great effect on *Rupert*'s eventual recovery and return home.

They had worked to gain access for children to their unconscious parents in intensive care, stressing the importance of children 'talking to mother, even if she seems to be asleep, and to touch her.'

June Jolly writes of a badly injured boy (12) who 'was completely unresponsive for four months. His family gave him daily bulletins on the family activities, his school friends visited, chatting round his bed; there was even a birthday celebrated over his inert body.' He regained consciousness and 'seemed to be quite in touch with reality. As he improved he was able to report all sorts of things he "remembered" from the time when no one else was aware he could hear, let alone understand. We can never be sure but we should never presume' (Jolly, 1981, p.68).

Music

June Jolly also recalls a boy (6) whom she nursed for many weeks making 'his first conscious movement in response to his favourite record' (Jolly, 1981, p.68).

The power and importance of music may easily be overlooked in the busy life of caring adults but increasingly with radio and recording, personal stereos and musak-filled supermarkets, we move like actors in films, surrounded by rhythm and melody counterpointing every action and emotion. Yet in only two of my visits, and little of my reading, was music mentioned and there were no instruments in playrooms. Probation officer Alec Grant referred to the achievement experienced by young offenders who attended an electronic music workshop and made their own tapes. Ann Harris (HV) described singing games with handicapped children.

Suffering toys

Reference has been made to animals as objects of love and as givers of comfort and aids to communication. These functions are mirrored in their representations as toys and in books. A small model owl appears importantly in Jean Little's story of two children whose father dies of cancer. Hoot, given to Jeremy by his father, fulfils many roles and has strong symbolic significance, for example, in relation to the real owl which the boy and his father have seen together.

When the father is to go to hospital Jeremy gives him Hoot. During a visit when the boy can find nothing to say 'that held meaning' his father shows how much he values the owl and therefore his son. After his father's death Jeremy's mother returns the owl.

> The minute his fingers recognized the small stone owl, he jerked his
> hand back as if it had burned him. The calm he had been building up
> so carefully, shattered. His breath came in ragged gasps. His hands
> tightened into fists. He was alone and his father was gone
>
> (Little, 1985, p.115).

A teddy bear was pressed into service by June Jolly and a 20-month-old child whose severely scalded hands and feet 'were hidden by huge occlusive bandages. It was a relief to learn that in fact one could easily show even such a tiny child that underneath those monstrous gloves her hands and feet were still there. By using a precious teddy, taking his paws and bandaging them over and over again, one could repeat "See, teddy's hand, see, teddy's foot is still there"' (1981, p.101).

Dolls too may suffer. George Eliot's Maggie had

> a fetish, which she punished for all her misfortunes ... the trunk of a

large wooden doll, which once stared with the roundest of eyes above
the reddest of cheeks, but was now entirely defaced by a long career of
vicarious suffering. Three nails driven into the head commemorated as
many crises in Maggie's nine years of earthly struggle. . . . Immediately
after the last nail had been driven in with a fiercer strike than usual, . . .
Maggie had reflected that if she drove many nails in, she would not be
so well able to fancy that the head was hurt when she knocked it against
the wall, nor to comfort it and make believe to poultice it when the fury
was abated . . .

(Eliot, 1979, pp.24–5).

An attractive animal character may be invaluable as the subject of a
story which charts the circumstances of the child's own life. *May* was
very fond of Winnie-the-Pooh, who had adventures undreamed of by
A. A. Milne. *Pearl* produced Pooh-type drawings as the bear acquired
and lost parents, siblings and foster homes. *May* could choose to
identify with the bear or not, she could add to the simple pictures and
contribute to the story. *Pearl* could speculate on Pooh's feelings and
show him being naughty and cross and sad, which were 'dangerous' for
May herself. The latest adventures of Pooh were usually narrated and
discussed in a cuddle.

Another animal assistant was *Jessie*, a woolly glove puppet. *May*
wanted to call her '*May*' but *Pearl* considered that three-way conversation in which two participants had the same name would be
disastrous. '*Jessie*' was *May*'s own second name. *Jessie* contributed by
joining in conversations, by being left outside because she was 'naughty',
and by being fun.

Writing about working with children is often short on fun. Despite
the difficulties of *May*'s life, she and *Pearl* found much to enjoy during
their sessions. *Rachel West* aimed to make coming into hospital 'fun'
and playrooms, for example, in Rownberry House, were cheerful and
bright. Perhaps we have not fully recognized the power of humour in
healing.

Jeremy's mother did remember that laughter can heal. After his
father's death, Jeremy could not sleep. Guessing that he was feeling
miserable, his mother

stuck her head in his bedroom door. 'Jeremy,' she said, 'what happened
when the canary flew into the blender?' He propped himself up on one
elbow, relief flooding through him. 'I don't know. What?' 'Shredded
tweet.'

(Little, 1985, p.64)

(Another animal suffers in the cause of healing!) The words don't
matter. The communication is in the recognition of the child's need,
the ability of the adult to hit the right note, the relief experienced.

Jeremy groaned loudly and fell back on his pillow. In three minutes flat, he fell asleep

(Little, 1985, p.64).

Frozen images

An important form of communication without, or together with words, is the photograph. So highly do we regard the visual record of ourselves and our lives that one bride restaged her wedding because the video of the genuine event was unsatisfactory.

Wedding photographs have such a particular power that we even pore over the pictures of radio actors portraying characters in a serial for example, *The Archers*: 'Elizabeth looked just right but surely Shula doesn't look like that!' Wedding photographs are strange masquerades frozen under gelatine. The whole of life is there. The wedding is the end of one story, the beginning of another. Most fascinating, perhaps, are the wedding photographs of our parents. Did my mother really look like that? Look at grandma's hat! Who's that little girl? Such photographs hold many clues. Freely displayed on mantlepieces and in cream and silver albums they may be admired, laughed at, ignored.

But hidden and hard to find, they may be dynamite. Alison Leonard has written a novel about Tina (15) who finds a photograph of her parents' wedding. Her mother is dead and no one will speak about her or give any information.

It's odd, you know, a photo, ... You've *got* the person, caught them in a net, and you think you can take them apart and gaze at every bit of them and get to understand them. But it's not like that. The longer you look at them the further away they seem to get. You can't ask them things, you can't find out what's going on inside them

(Leonard, 1988, pp.29–30).

The main clues are a bridesmaid whose chin identifies her as Tina's aunt and the name and address of the photographer, which Tina uses to find her aunt and the truth. Her mother committed suicide when she could no longer bear her illness; Huntington's Chorea.

The photograph has set off a time bomb, as does the wedding picture of Kate's parents in *The Way to Sattin Shore*, which is also the way to Kate's discovery of her lost father and confused identity.

Under folded scarves and squares in a drawer lay an old photograph album and wedding photograph of twenty years ago: the wedding of Catharine Randall to Frederick Tranter. She studied the face of Frederick Tranter: she could not tell whether her face was like it ....

(Pearce, 1985, p.97)

It is possible for children in the 1990s to see photographs of ancestors as far back as great-great-great-great-grandparents. What do we find in those faces and figures which eventually became ourselves? For many people, identifying personal and family history is of immense importance. People spend years and small fortunes tracing family trees through registers and graveyards, documents and photographs.

May's most precious possession was her photograph album. Hardly a week passed without her looking through the pictures with *Pearl*. Each picture was greeted with the enthusiasm of fresh discovery. The only face she could study for signs of likeness to her own was her own. Even then the photographs spanned only two years. To be able to say 'That's me, that's the jumper I'm wearing now. That's my birthday party,' was invaluable for a child whose sense of self, her place in time and space and in relation to other people was almost non-existent. In order to focus on *May*'s life as a small baby *Pearl* cut photographs from magazines; it was difficult to explain the difference between a real picture of *May* and one of someone who was like her.

Photographs may attain immense importance as symbols, representing, for example, the reality of missing parents. For Gilly Hopkins (real name Galadriel) beginning life, in Katherine Paterson's novel, in her third foster home in less than three years (the Dixons had moved to Florida and Mrs Richmond had to go into hospital 'for her nerves'), the photograph of her mother represents the one link with what Gilly feels to be her real self.

> Out of the pasteboard frame and through the plastic cover the brown eyes of the woman laughed up at her as they always did. The glossy black hair hung in gentle waves without a hair astray. She looked as though she was the star of some TV show, but she wasn't. See – right there in the corner she had written 'For my beautiful Galadriel, I will always love you.' She wrote that to me, Gilly told herself, as she did each time she looked at it, only to me. She turned the frame over. It was still there – the little piece of tape with the name on it. 'Courtney Rutherford Hopkins.' Gilly smoothed her own straw-coloured hair with one hand as she turned the picture over again. Even the teeth were gorgeous. Weren't girls supposed to look like their mothers? The word 'mother' triggered something deep in her stomach
>
> (Paterson, 1981, pp.9, 16–17).

The real Courtney, when eventually Gilly meets her, is a terrible disappointment. Only her teeth resemble her portrait and she certainly does not love her 'beautiful Galadriel'. But by then Gilly no longer needs the transitional object of the photograph. She can manage real life.

June Jolly draws attention to children in hospitals who need to realize that 'Mummy will come tomorrow'. 'Younger children can be helped to retain an image of Mummy if she is asked to leave some tangible evidence of herself, such as a glove or handbag. For older children a photograph to keep on the locker will provide a focus so nurses and other staff can talk with the child about his family' (Jolly, 1981, pp.88–9).

How many of us keep photographs of our partners and children on desks and in wallets? How we use pictures and videos of holidays and babies and family events as a focus for talking about ourselves. It sometimes seems that an event or place or person exists only if a photographic record is made.

It seems too that we sometimes engage in exciting experiences in order to collect memories. Oliver, a young boy in a novel reflects 'I shall always have this escapade to look back on'

(Taylor,1988, p. 118).

Photographs may be invaluable not only for discovering the past and recording the present but also for helping to prepare for the future. Some foster parents prepare albums of photographs about themselves and their home to leave with prospective foster children.

Lily and Albert Foreman wrote that the new foster parents came to talk to us ... to get the feel of how the children lived. They left a book of photos and stories about themselves for the children to see.' The children, 'looked at the book and at the family that we had talked about for so long' (Foreman, L. and A., 1985, pp.54–5). The photographs formed a bridge between the initial anxiety about abstract unknown and unwanted foster parents and the first meeting with people who must then begin to become real and to make demands. The photographs showed real people but still safe, frozen onto the paper, controllable.

A very different and disturbing comment on photographs is given by Beatrix Campbell. A picture of sexually abused children:

> invites us into the shocking realization that the child has been sexualized because it is an object. In the pin-up the woman is made an object for the male spectator because she is sexual, but in both genres, the subjectivity of the child and the woman alike is denied by the *presence* of the *absence* – the viewer or, in this context, the abuser.
> The evidential photographs of abused anuses and vulvas are more than painful – and that they are: they are troubling. They are sexual because they are defined not just by the child's body but by the invisible presence of the perpetrator. They are difficult pictures to see because what they show is not only a body but a relationship. They may cause you grief or they may work on your fantasies, but either way, you have to work out who you are as you watch, if you are to know what to think
> (Campbell, 1988, p.81).

This draws attention to one of the most difficult areas with which any of us may be called to work. But it also identifies the need for constant vigilance over our responses to the stimuli inevitably and often unpalatably offered in work with children. Photographs may seem to be contained, controlled, remote. But even the most innocuous-seeming may be smiling grenades, and not only for the child.

Summary

Messages are given and received in many ways, often unconsciously. It is essential to attend to all signs and clues and to seek balance. Waiting, and protecting children from pressure, may be a powerful form of communication. But adults may, for a variety of reasons, be content with wrong interpretations of children's messages. All communication is two-way and begins at the beginning of life. Various means of and aids to communication are explored: crying, smiling, physical comfort, cuddling, animals and birds, communicating with unconscious people, music, toys, photographs.

Link

Almost all the illustrations given in this and preceding chapters have been of ordinary everyday activities and materials. Even when the context is death or illness, move of home or confusion about identity, communication is through loving interaction between adult and child, without elaborate equipment. Communication is everyday and, as illustrated in Chapter 10, everyminute.

10   Everyminute communication

Everyminute communication

Reviewing a book on access, John Pierson misses 'the texture and density of everyday work' (1989, p.42).

Almost everything described in the present book is everyday, not least because the circumstances which invite attention of adult professional helpers are the everyday life of the child: illness, handicap, abuse, move from home. Too much elaboration and equipment can obstruct clear, simple communication.

Helen King does not believe in 'a great deal of plant. Use yourself and what's in your handbag. You can get all the information with the contents of your handbag.' Such everyday equipment as pencils and paper may help to achieve better communication than any number of special dolls.

Sharing ordinary activity may lead to confidence and understanding. Alfred Torrie writes that a 'child who shared in his father's gardening enthusiasm realized something of the cycle of life and change which never stops. This helped to make clear the value of decay which in fact fed new life' (Torrie, 1978, p.11).

Communicating with children is not only everyday and ordinary but everyminute and constant. *Nancy Mint* and *Elaine Kent* regard everyminute communication as fundamental. Many children attending the family centre have been or are suspected of having been, subject to sexual abuse. 'It's accepted by courts and so on that if the child is to disclose sexual abuse it should be to police or social workers. But these may not be people the child knows and trusts and feels secure with. A lot may be disclosed but in the right circumstances.'

The right circumstances include time and the ability to attend so thoroughly to the child that every message is received and understood. *Elaine* found that she was so engrossed in sessions with *Lucy* that after one meeting she was unable to remember what had been said. With *Lucy*'s permission *Nancy* thereafter acted as scribe.

Working with children may involve special contacts between designated adults and troubled children in planned contexts with prepared methods, particular places and pre-determined time limits. Whatever the impact of such contacts, total contact time must represent very little of the children's life-time, during which they are in contact with many other people.

For almost all children, the most important people with whom they have regular everyday contact are their peers: other children in the playground, the gang, best friends. Adult carers are important but, unless things go wrong, can be taken for granted as providers, fulfillers of functions.

To avoid confusion *Joanna* encouraged her stepdaughter to use her first name. One weekend *Rosie* (6) kept calling her 'Mummy'. Earnestly *Joanna* took *Rosie* on her knee: 'I'm not your Mummy, I'm your friend. I look after you when you're in this house.' *Rosie* was perfectly aware of this and of the roles of all the confused adults in her life. Kindly she explained, 'When I'm here you do the things mummies do.' Only the adults were worried about the rivalries and confusion. *Rosie* herself was perfectly clear.

On an occasion when she wasn't clear and had to find her way between wanting to live with her father but not wanting to leave her mother's home, communication took place largely on the bathroom floor, *Rosie* cuddled onto *Joanna*'s knee because the conversation had started at bathtime. *Rosie*'s eventual decision to remain with her mother was made not as a choice between adults, for she wanted everyone, but because she did not want to leave her toy cupboard or school friends. The idea of transferring toys and making new friends was too difficult and probably inappropriate. In emotional turmoil *Rosie* identified and clung to the aspects of her life which had most solidity and relevance.

Most people make their adult homes with others of their own, not their parents' generation and most set a great store by toy cupboards containing cars, kitchen equipment, gardening tools, and dressing-up boxes.

Clothing

Clothes and appearance are a constant and often overlooked, however much looked-at, means of communication and play important roles in legends and fairy stories.

Cinderella can go to the ball only when suitably and magically clad and her lost slipper provides the only clue to her identity. Cap o'Rushes, a Cinderella-Cordelia figure rejected by her Lear-type father, becomes both known and disguised by her garment, a cape of rushes.

The heroine of *East of the Sun, West of the Moon* (a version of the Psyche myth), trades glorious dresses, products of three magic nuts, for three nights with the Prince whom she must convince that she is his true wife.

Epic battles have been fought over school uniform, *Warren* insisted on wearing a woolly hat to school, a challenge to assert his rather bizarre individuality and a medium for a battle of wills between father and head.

In 1990 two Muslim girls were readmitted to school after a period of exclusion due to their determination to wear headscarves in obedience to Islamic custom. Compromise was reached when they were permitted to wear scarves in the uniform navy blue.

Beryl Bainbridge's Alice knows about clothes as communicators.

> The night before the funeral there were the usual threats about how I needn't think I was going to wear my jeans and duffle coat. I didn't argue. She knew perfectly well I was going to wear them
> (Bainbridge, 1980, p.60).

I went to school with boys from a children's home who were dressed in grey flannel long-shorts, their white locknit underpants dangling to the knee. We called them 'the homes boys'. Children in hospital used to be put into hospital clothes because, said *Rachel West*, 'Staff couldn't take responsibility for their own' which were sent home. The hospital clothes were a motley collection and passed from child to child so that they 'looked as if they came from an orphanage'.

Now children wear their own clothes and are no longer bathed on arrival with implications of being dirty. Babies who die are dressed in their own clothes while parents hold them and grieve. They are buried in those clothes and with a toy.

Much of our identity is expressed in our clothing: prettiness, neatness, choice of colour, styling for ease of activity, toughness for heavy duty. Taking away our chosen coverings as in prison is a form of de-personalization, an aid to control.

Jane Aldgate and Janet Galley record that Joyce (17), fostered by her aunt and uncle, expressed some of her confusion about her identity and future through ordering then cancelling then re-ordering new clothes (Aldgate and Galley, 1988, p.69). Who was she? What personality was being clothed? What identity expressed? Joyce had control over very few aspects of her life. Now she was to make choices on such important matters as whether to be adopted by her relations and future training and employment.

For children with a physical handicap the ability not only to choose but to care for clothes and even more to dress and undress signifies control. Nicola Madge and Meg Fassam record the words of a girl (15) with spina bifida on getting dressed. 'My dad used to do it up to when I was about 12 when one day I said, "No, I've got fed up with this, I'll do it myself now." So he stood and watched me do it, then he let me do it on my own. . . .' Until she was 12 'my mum was washing my hair and ironing my clothes. Then one day I thought "This is a bit stupid, she can't do it all my life so I might as well do it myself." So one day she went out, and when she came back I'd ironed all the clothes and she said "Cor, you're getting good"' (Madge and Fassam, 1982, p.36).

Through the sensible responses of her parents this girl was helped towards independence; secure in their care she could take risks, including giving up some aspects of being cared-for.

For children in residential care, feeling cared-for may have more significance than details of day-to-day care. Ruth Gardner met Jamey (14) for whom 'the purchase of clothes provided a memory of parental care: "My dad opened a Co-op account for us before he died – sometimes I get clothes from that." '

For boys in a community home with education the activity of shopping provided an opportunity for interaction with a particular staff member. They 'preferred to buy clothes with the only female member of staff if they could not go with a relation – perhaps because this felt more like an ordinary family outing than "supervision". There was some evidence that, although teenage boys felt rather silly asking for help with clothes and food they needed and appreciated the help given ...' (Gardner, 1987, p.37).

Children have so little control over their lives, so few real decisions. Clothing provides opportunity to offer choice and show care. Tove Jansson illustrates both in a story about Ninny who, abused and invisible, is boarded out with the Moomin family.

> 'How on earth does one make her visible again,' Moomin-pappa said worriedly. 'Should we take her to a doctor?' 'I don't think so,' said Moominmamma. 'I believe that she wants to be invisible for a while'
>
> (1973, p.108).

When eventually Ninny's paws and legs have emerged

> one could see the faint outline of a brown dress hem. [Later] Moominmamma took out a rose-pink shawl of hers and made it into a little dress.... Then she made a broad hair ribbon out of material left over.... The following day Ninny had her dress on. She was visible up to her neck, ... and piped 'Thank you all ever so much'
>
> (p.112).

A pretty dress and un-pressing care enable the hiding child to risk revealing more of herself.

Many children are 'invisible'. *Rachel West* recalled *Natalie* (6) in hospital following non-accidental injury. She 'wouldn't communicate, smile, talk or eat. Just sat in her cot. She wouldn't even go to the toilet. Staff worked on a one-to-one basis. I was there all weekend. On the Monday she came out of the bathroom holding out her dress, saying "Don't I look pretty!" ' Both *Ninny* and *Natalie* rewarded the caring adults with recovery.

Care

Attention to children's welfare entails every aspect of physical, emotional, spiritual and social care. Concern and its lack may be shown in many ways and may represent and communicate far more than the small act of care, or withholding. Jocelyn Maximé and Asrat-Girma illustrate the devastating interaction between faulty social attitudes, intolerant environments and physical care. Morris (5), a black child in residential care was losing his hair 'from lack of care and he was told that he was not black.' When Jocelyn Maximé visited the home, he told her not to 'refer to him as black, after observing me speaking with the head of the home. However, he did not realize that I had come with a black social worker.... Thinking she was a possible parent and not connected with the authority, he ran to her begging her to take him away, talking positively about black people and himself to her' (Maximé, 1986, p.103). Such assault on the child's self-image is not confined to race and skin colour. For example the 'wrong' regional accent may stimulate ridicule and even contempt.

Asrat-Girma found the day care nurseries she studied in 12 London boroughs 'invariably dominated by inflexible routines and standardized views of child care and child development, which were often at odds with those of the parents and yet which were never open to negotiation.' For example, 'West Indian parents had often tried to explain the difficulty of getting sand out of their children's hair, yet the staff reaction typically was 'Coloured parents don't like their children to get dirty ... some of them even ask that their children be not allowed to play with sand or water....'' '

She recalls 'an Asian child whose parents had put a certain type of cream on her hair which was promptly washed off by the staff when she entered the nursery, on the grounds that it was "smelly"' (Asrat-Girma, 1986, p.44).

Syble Morgan recommends that nursery nurse training 'be changed to reflect the reality of our multi-cultural society'. This would include information about 'black hair and skin care.... It is very important that black children in social services run nurseries are given Afro-Caribbean foods, and are taught respect for the value their ancestors must have placed on this part of their culture, so that through practice and oral traditions they pass it on' (Morgan, 1986, pp.73–4).

Food

Syble Morgan advises that attention be given to foods and eating practices; like clothing and other forms of physical care these are crucial but easily overlooked aspects of everyday communication.

In numerous legends food is dangerous. Powerful themes are the perversion of everyday caring, and danger hidden in outward seeming wholesomeness.

In the Snow White story, for example, the wicked queen and step-mother manufactured an apple that was deadly poison. Outwardly it looked so beautiful and tempting with its rosy cheek that every one who saw it must long to taste it .... When the apple was ready she painted her face and got herself up to look like a farmer's wife' (Grimm, p.204).

The images of rosy apple and farmer's wife, superficially wholesome but inwardly lethal, counterpoint the themes of the good birth mother who deserts the child by dying, and the replacement of another mother who tries to kill, using the very currency of care, food.

In the work of child psychotherapist Margaret Hunter with Julia (7), a 'frozen' child, Snow White plays an important part. Before being committed to care as a baby and fostered at three Julia had been starved. She 'vividly enacted the cruel stepmother's attempt to kill Snow White but told me: "Only in this story she doesn't win and Snow White is queen."'

In one session she begged for food but Margaret Hunter decided not to feed her, feeling that 'it was important to empathize with her hunger but not interpret it materially; she was no longer starving physically but psychically and this hunger could only be fed with understanding.'

Really attending to a child in such pain and need may have tremen-dous impact on the worker. Doll 'babies were made to put their heads into the toilet to eat their food whilst she laughed and sneered at them.' Margaret Hunter, 'had a sudden terrible realization that I was about to be sick. I had forcibly to distract myself for a few moments. The feeling passed and I was again able to talk with her about a mother who bears babies but does not feed them, who forces them to resort to a toilet for food, to their own waste products because the life-giving milk is withheld.'

After three years of twice weekly work which owed much also to the foster parents and social worker, Julia was 'on her way to becoming [a] "real girl" at last' (Hunter, 1987, pp.28, 30).

Unaccustomed food, however wholesome, may act like poison. In *Goodnight Mister Tom*, William is half starved by his mother. Evacuated to a village, he is placed with Mister Tom who provides plenty of simple, good food. But after William's birthday party,

'The excitement and food simply welled up inside him and he gave a short gasp and vomited all over the carpet.'

(Magorian, 1983, p.115).

Mister Tom, who eventually adopts him, communicates perfectly. He simply clears up the mess. Social worker *Lyn Verrall* took *Josie* (12) to visit the foster home where she had first lived after reception into care, as part of life-story work. Because she had been suffering from malnutrition when first placed she had been given a special diet. But at Christmas she 'stole' a piece of turkey and was sick all over the table. The foster mother's tolerance and this vivid picture of herself helped *Josie* in her discovery of her history.

Asrat-Girma found that 'The kinds of food on offer, alien to several of the ethnic groups in the nursery, were given on a "take it or leave it" basis, or, worse, were forced upon children ... a Filipino child who consistently refused to eat boiled vegetables, had been force-fed, and vomited constantly. She missed out on her desserts in an effort by staff to make her eat the undesired food' (Asrat-Girma, 1986, p.43).

Lack of understanding of the everyday life of other people can lead to dangerous interpretations and misdirected practice: 'one senior worker with experience of working with Asian women in an intensive care unit suggested that babies she was dealing with were under-weight because their parents ate curry!' (p.44).

Ruth Gardner found similar lack of understanding and tolerance in some residential establishments. One boy said, 'I don't mean to be rude or anything. I just can't eat pork. I've never eaten it, but every time they serve it or any fried food I feel sick and they think I'm messing about' (Gardner, 1987, p.33).

For many people food has religious or philosophical significance and to be forced, for whatever reason, to renège on such beliefs and practices hinders integration, inter- or intra-personal. Nessa (17) came from a Bangladeshi family. Her white keyworker said that she had 'rejected the Muslim faith and its requirement, at times, of a vegetarian diet. Nessa, on the other hand, said she did eat with her family whenever she was with them, but it was difficult to cook Muslim food for one in a residential home ... the main reason for her eating Western convenience foods' (p.33).

Why does anyone have to eat convenience foods in a residential home? Is not an essential part of living together and learning how to become healthy and independent the selection and preparation of good, fresh food?

Ruth Gardner recognizes that 'It is clearly impossible for everyone's preferences to be met consistently. Some catering staff in residential establishments *did* consult young people regularly and managed so that individuals did not have to eat what they hated, while ... "favourite" dishes were provided, from time to time ...' (p.32).

Asrat-Girma found little tolerance for table manners: 'Children were never allowed to use their fingers to eat with, irrespective of the cultures from which they came' (p.43).

Mealtimes can become a battleground in the happiest family; how much more fraught when there is stress. *Rosie*'s last meal of a visit used to be hell on earth, the focus for all the tensions about leaving her father and returning to her mother felt by herself, her father and her stepmother *Joanna*. The adults eventually realized that *Rosie* and *Joanna*, having been happy and loving together throughout the visit, contrived to have a row over the meal so that they could manage the parting in terms of 'Thank goodness I'm going/she's gone', submerging the pain in anger and relief.

Following overnight stays with his parents over a number of weeks, prior to return home, *Wayne* (4) caused much frustration to his foster parents by refusing to eat.

Food may combine opportunities for communication on several levels at a time. When Sarah Mumford bought James a hamburger, presumably James himself chose the food so had the opportunity to exercise some control in a world which largely if not entirely controlled him. Going to the shop provided a new neutral focus for an outing and he had more control over choosing where to eat. The gift of food identified Sarah as a caring nourishing adult. Her ability to allow junk food showed her as flexible and attuned to the boy (Banks and Mumford, 1988, pp.108–9).

Philippa Pearce shows Kate trying, often desperately, to gain attention from her mother to help with her anxiety about her apparently dead father and her own sense of identity. 'She wanted to talk to her mother when her mother had been making pastry,' a comfortable everyday activity providing the opportunity for sharing, distraction and the avoidance of eye contact. But 'she had not been able to.' In bed,

> Kate clutched at her mother; but she still could not say the things she had to say .... She wept and wept. 'I'm so hungry. I didn't have any tea ....' [Her mother offers to get some food but] Kate wept more than ever, because what she – Kate – had said was not at all what she needed to say. Not at all.
>
> [Her mother recognizes that there is more to tell but wisely provides food first,] 'a steaming bowl of bread and milk, and a spoon to eat it with' [which mother made sometimes] if one of her children were not well. The milk had to be very hot, but not boiled; the bread torn up into small fragments; and there must be a little salt and a little nutmeg and a lot – oh! a lot – of sugar, ...
>
> (Pearce, 1985, pp.82–3).

The mother at last attends to all the needs of her daughter, not distracted from the physical by the evidence of emotional distress but offering sustenance and comfort to the whole child. The special nursery food indicates that she is aware that Kate needs special attention; she gives thought and time to its preparation; she brings it to and stays with the troubled little girl.

The importance of a meal as part of a ritual indicating continuing identity within a group has significance for working with children.

Love in little things

Roles in even the most homely ritual may be significant. Elizabeth Taylor describes a little girl sitting in a cafe

> with her father and two younger children. When the tea was brought, her father nodded at her with a casual and flattering gesture. Colour rose up in her cheeks. She stood up and lifted the tea-pot with two hands .... [Her father] so apparently relaxed, was ready to spring to her rescue. The wobbly stream of tea descended into his cup. He took it from her with careless thanks. She smiled. She shone with relief. 'This is my first time,' she said, 'of pouring out.'

An observer thinks ' "Love is not difficult," .... In the child's father it had seemed the simplest thing, as was the expression of it' (Taylor, 1986, p.236). In this novel, as in so much of life, love seems to be very difficult indeed, perhaps because we try too hard and look for too much.

Love is often expressed best in little things. D. June Ellis recalled learning this during her first week in a residential teaching post in a boarding school when 'a girl ran away leaving notes all the way up the stairs, "Don't follow me Miss Ellis." Of course, I did follow her but I could not get her in the car and came back to Jonas Fielding (a senior colleague, also in residence) to explain. There was nothing more we could do, not a lesson I liked learning, because activity is infinitely preferable to inactivity in times of stress.'

Eventually the girl was found in the village and Jonas Fielding took June Ellis to collect her. 'When we returned to my study he said to her "Miss Ellis will make you a cup of tea" – my reaction was "What, me, make her a cup of tea when I've just been dragged out of bed." However, ... I made the tea and I don't even drink it myself!'

June Ellis realized that, 'the time taken for us all to calm down and for us to meet a little more closely, over that refreshment, was a turning-point for that girl who went from strength to strength but not before she had run away several more times and I had made other cups of tea. That small thing was very important ...' (1981, pp.5–6).

Cups of tea and coffee can help to set boundaries. Making and serving and drinking define a basic period of time of which the child can be sure. They also provide regular events which can be anticipated. *May*'s foster mother always prepared a tray containing teapot, milk jug, sugar, two cups and saucers and a plate of biscuits. Serving the tea was a little way in which *Pearl* could show care, while *May* allocated biscuits, making sure that both she and *Pearl* had one each of every variety. Both *Pearl* and *May* enjoyed the care shown by the foster mother.

Even at the (very slight) risk of breakage it was important to *May*'s gradually increasing self-confidence that she should be trusted to help, just as Elizabeth Taylor's little girl grew so much because her father, although ready to spring to her rescue, was so apparently relaxed. No paralysing 'do be careful, dear' or 'don't scald yourself.' Trust communicated in little things increases trust.

Little things are important in hospital too. Dave J. Müller *et al.* propose 'thoughtful touches, such as fastening a name to a child's doll. These increase children's feelings of being a person rather than a condition and add a bit of harmless fun to the whole experience' (Müller *et al.*, 198, p.146).

But little things can be equally distressing. Müller refers to a boy (11) who was given a too-small operating gown. 'A nurse told him that she would get another, but after half an hour came back to say she could not find another one. He kept asking if he could put a blanket around him to go to the toilet, but a nurse said she would bring a bed pan instead, which made him more embarrassed since he was being teased by younger children in the ward already' (p.134).

What other equipment might be inadequate and with no satisfactory replacement? The small matter of the small gown might stimulate not only embarrassment and discomfort but also anxiety and fear. It could certainly not foster trust.

Asrat-Girma identified little things with considerable negative impact in many of the nurseries she visited which 'had no policy of meeting the needs of any of the ethnic groups represented in terms of play, reading materials, music, storytelling, food, and so on. In fact, books were found such as *Little Black Sambo* which are downright offensive to black children. The Robertson's jam golliwog was also 'greatly in evidence' and was justified by a nursery worker 'on the grounds that she as a white person had always loved the toy as a "nice friendly creature"' (Asrat-Girma pp.43, 44–5).

"Little" insensitivities of this kind can communicate at least lack of understanding, and more likely indifference or deliberate hostility.

In their study of children with physical disabilities Madge and Fassam found that lack of imagination about little things could inhibit integration: 'practical difficulties faced by disabled children trying to collect several items of food and cutlery in the school dining room, while attempting to maintain their balance or manage aids, had led to the practice of putting all these pupils at one table.' Instead of moving towards independence and minimizing the effects of disability, the children were identified as different and un-able and felt 'resentment and frustration' (Madge and Fassam, 1982, p.147).

In contrast, boys taking part in the *Boundless Project* gained confidence through taking responsibility for planning, purchasing and preparing food for weekends in the hills.

Environment: the child

In Philippa Pearce's novel, Kate's mother provided not only food and understanding. Once she recognized her daughter's desperate need she created a whole environment of comfort and intimacy, including refusing to answer demands from any other member of her household. No amount of apology when the telephone or a caller interrupt can erase the disruption or reinstate the sense of inviolate times and space essential to any real interaction. How can you repose confidence in someone who, with however much expressed regret and discomfort, can divert from your story to discuss another client or the date of some meeting, with an intruder?

When Kate had been given her special supper her mother brought in an electric blow-heater. Mrs Tranter plugged it in, shut the door, drew the curtains and switched off the light

> so that the room was in darkness for a moment, and Kate stopped eating her bread and milk. [Then she] turned the heater on: besides blowing out hot air, it gave a red glow to the room.
>
> [They] were shut into a safe, warm, reddish gloom of light. She could just see to eat ... [and] the dark shape of her mother sitting on the edge of the bed, close to her. Against one of Kate's legs lay a heavy weight of contentment: the dozing Syrup. [Mrs Tranter's careful arrangement means that Kate can reveal her anxieties without eye contact.] Now they faced each other; but in that warm dusk neither could see the other's face clearly. It was easier for them so
>
> (Pearce, 1985, pp.83, 84).

The environment not only aids or inhibits but is itself communication. Mrs Tranter created an environment which communicated attention and affection. Reduction of visible space created focus and security.

May and *Pearl* always met in the foster home. *Pearl* took an old tablecloth to protect the carpet from glue and crumbs. This became an island, a focus of their shared space.

Sarah Mumford tried to work with Lennox (7), 'in his cramped bedroom. Not surprisingly this was unsatisfactory.' Eventually she and her supervisor 'agreed that she would take him to the park once a week. Now she cannot stop Lennox talking!' (Banks and Mumford, 1988, p.107). The ability to alter the setting of contact communicated that Sarah was really attending to the boy and prepared to change her routine to help him.

Divorce court welfare officers were conscious of the different messages which may be given and received in diverse settings. While the office could be inhibiting because of strangeness, contact in a neutral setting, away from the homes of disputing parents, would be essential. Children would be seen in both houses too but *Laura Bridge* disliked talking to children in either home because of 'the sense of listening parents'. The highly charged message of the home environments could influence the child even if the parent were not present.

Learning about children at home is essential to making assessments. Everyminute communication includes not only physical conditions but also unconscious messages which are constantly exchanged. Social worker Roger Lake, assessing the behaviour of Clifford (5) and his relationship with his mother Yvonne, deliberately visited at a mealtime. 'Clifford was in a tetchy mood, unable to settle at the table, hurling cutlery around, and shouting that he wanted to watch TV. Despite his remonstrations, he eventually ate his food with little fuss.'

Roger Lake noted that, 'the measures to discipline Clifford were inconsistent and dependent on his mother's moods. "Bedroom" was a punishment, as was "smacking" .... Yvonne spoke of how Clifford's physical appearance and behaviour had reminded her so much of his father that she sometimes had nightmares that he was "mad, just like his father"' (Adcock, Lake and Small, 1988, pp.32–3). The everyminute communication of being present as everyday life proceeded was revealing.

Workers in health and social care often endeavour to improve the home environment. *Ellen Barnes* describes the aim of her family centre as 'to create an environment which helps them to look up but which is attainable.'

The particular environment is the sitting room in a unit with kitchen and bathroom but *Ellen*'s words stand for the philosophy of the whole centre. The unit was furnished to provide a comfortable and practical setting for play, discussion, family therapy and learning practical skills. *Ellen* drew attention to the walls, papered with woodchip and colour washed so that not only could repairs be cheap and easy but also families could learn ways of improving dingy rooms under attack from greasy-fingered children. Looking up is all very well but it must be to something attainable or despair may deepen.

Environment: the worker

Communication confined to the worker's own time and territory is exhausting. How much more so when in a family centre workers may be exposed for considerable periods and not necessarily to their 'own' clients.

Ellen Barnes understands the importance of messages given by the total environment to both clients and workers. 'The staff must feel supported and cared for to go on giving out.' What messages are conveyed to troubled people by 'helpers' who are perpetually tired, harassed and late? 'How can you help families not to break down at the risk of the worker's families breaking down?

Recently returned to work after a serious illness she felt very well supported by the line management of her employing voluntary society. This she could pass on to her staff, helping to create the environment of everyminute caring and encouragement so desperately needed by the client families.

The comment of Dave J. Müller *et al.* on the hospital environment is applicable to all settings. 'Staff and parents need to be able to get along well together and for this to happen both parents and nurses need their own "territory"; a place to which they can retreat and relax' (Müller *et al.*, 1986, p.108).

How unlike the messages given by noisy open-plan offices in which anxious and weary social workers are expected to think, discuss, plan, record, telephone. Small chance of finding retreat and relaxation when sandwiches are eaten at desks in five minutes between appointments.

Muriel, who showed great commitment by attending an evening course for social workers and foster parents together, commented sadly that she could rarely undertake the kind of direct work with children being discussed because an emergency would arise or a meeting be called. *Ben* asked how to persuade senior staff that spending time with children was not 'skiving'.

Some of Cleveland's problems developed from lack of consideration between working specialists. Once diagnosed as abused by doctor Marietta Higgs children were often admitted to the paediatric wards but a nurse commented that: 'None of these children were ill and they treated the ward like a playgroup, going out on bikes, playing with their parents – and we had to amuse them for 18 hours a day. They'd play with the traction or play, literally, with the bed of a very sick child.'

Nurses 'found it hard to get information from [Marietta Higgs] on how long the children would be staying or what to do with them. They needed supervision. It was a nightmare' (Campbell, 1988, p.44).

Children and parents already intolerably anxious must have been further confused by these strange messages. Why were healthy children confined to hospital? How could a 'place of safety' be an overcrowded, inadequately staffed ward? And how did the sick children and their parents feel about this invasion?

Environment: the family

The Müller extract (above) refers to parents in the hospital setting. The family itself is a powerful environment engaged in everyminute communication. Else Stenbak writes, 'the trauma of an illness in one member will always affect the other members and their relationships. Parents can easily transmit their emotions to their child, so if the parents are calm and trustful the child will often be the same ... parents' emotional wellbeing ... has a positive effect on the child's recovery' (Stenbak, 1986, p.3).

Rachel West emphasizes the importance of 'treating the family. You can't treat a child in isolation.' She likes 'parents to be involved with care as much as possible but there is no pressure.' Care of the child includes care of the parent and it may be necessary to 'tell them that they're looking tired and give "permission" for them to leave the ward.'

Environment: social attitudes

The environment of social attitude is a powerful form of everyminute communication. Syble Morgan considers it vital for black children to be 'exposed to situations where black adults exert authority, leadership, initiative and knowledge to combat beliefs that they are inferior to whites' and 'taught to love themselves and other black people, as the basis for a loving personality in general' and 'to respect and love other ethnic groups as well' (Morgan, 1986, p.69–70).

Creating and maintaining a loving accepting environment is a fundamental aim of all work with and on behalf of children. Mike Mennell describes the positive messages gently conveyed to James (5) of mixed parentage by his white foster mother who, 'constantly introduced music, food, magazines and "ethnic" comics into the home and had made extra efforts to ensure that her social life (and that of James) included black people. Living in a predominantly white area of Bradford, where racist comment is an everyday factor at play and at school,' and helping him 'begin to counter racist taunting amongst his peers' (Mennell, 1986, p.131).

The use of environment as part of helping communication is relevant to every agency and setting. Dave J. Müller *et al.* advise that 'Small changes such as pictures on the walls, bright colours, a kettle for parents, an air freshener to disguise the hospital smell, and the arrangement of furniture to encourage communication can make a big difference' (Müller *et al.*, 1986, p.146).

Else Stenbak describes hospitals in nine countries including one with 'No visits allowed: average length of stay two weeks; toys in cupboards; infants tied at both hands and feet, to prevent them from spoiling their surgery .... Two children age three or four years each in a corner with their backs to the corridor silently rubbing their hands against the wall' (Stenbak, 1986, p.42).

Fortunately, in another country she visited 'A hospital with wallpaper; different colours, different animals for different ages; pictures low where children could see them; special lounge for adolescents, away from play room; apparently constantly contacting nurse; nursing care plans; cubicles for smaller children, all with a bed and a cupboard for mothers: overheard remark that it was necessary to have the parents here' (p.40).

The open window

Janusz Korczak understands how children communicate every-minute:

> The children are free to enter my room. We have an agreement: you can play, or talk in half-tones, or there must be absolute silence. I have a small chair, armchair and stool for my guests. There are three windows next each other; the middle one is open; the windows are low – thirty centimetres above the floor. For many years, every day I have placed the chair, the armchair and the stool far from the open window, sometimes I hide them somewhere in the corner. But every evening they are always back by the open window. Sometimes I notice that they move them with a decisive push, sometimes they lift them quietly and carefully, almost stealthily. Usually I do not know how it has happened. I put illustrated periodicals in different places, make access to the window difficult with flowerpots. And I am glad to see how ingeniously they resist the temptations to remove the obstacles; the open window wins – even when it is windy, when it is raining, when it is cold.
>
> The tropism which makes water plants grow here or there, upwards and downwards to crystallization, to chemical relationship – dictating this and not that compound; the law that makes potato shoots climb up the wall of the cellar towards the window grating above – and the same urge which, despite human rules, draw the prisoner to the window to look out into space.
>
> Children need movement, air, light – true, but also something else. They must look into space, get the feeling of freedom symbolised by the open window
>
> (Korczak, 1926–7: in Szlązakowa, p.42).

Summary

Communicating with children (or with adults) must be clear and simple, based on shared activity and everyday equipment. Some everyminute means of communication are explored, including clothing, care, food, little things, and the environment itself, including space and setting, the worker's environment, the family, and social attitudes. Everyminute communication is expressed in the room of Janusz Korczak, who wrote, and exemplified in his life, *How to Love a Child*.

Conclusion

England 1990. *Andrew* stands by his bed. His mother stands beside him saying goodbye. She says she will return tomorrow. He does not look at her. She does not touch him. He raises a limp hand in sad parody of a wave. The nurse, present throughout the scene, leaves with the mother and joins other nurses. *Andrew* stands, gazing at the floor. He has been admitted for surgery tomorrow.

I am amazed, hurt. I have almost finished writing this book, and, influenced by all that I have learned, I expect to see a nurse spring to his side offering understanding and occupation. The ward is brightly painted, there are cheerful curtains and copious books and toys. But *Andrew* is alone.

At last, unable to bear his withdrawal, I interfere – speak to him, bring him to join the child I am visiting, find him a book and ask him to read to me. When I leave, I draw the attention of nurses to him. I feel like a busybody, but they have not, before, attended to him.

In the course of writing *Attending to Children* I was engaged in direct social work with several children and found my philosophy and values well tested but also confirmed, both in this work and in contact with practitioners in other fields.

It isn't easy. But it is I believe the only way. To meet children and adults with honesty and respect, to face fear and seek truth, to trust and be trust-worthy, to risk and offer love. Focus must be on the whole person, not on a symptom or problem. Care must be shown in really listening and waiting, in support and encouragement and the development of self-confidence and esteem in both children and workers.

In order to work effectively and to pay the cost, workers need training and preparation and the same kind of listening and respect they offer the children.

Do not be seduced along alleys of elaboration of theory, language and equipment. Do not worry about complicated plans and reports. Do not be afraid of failing or looking foolish. Your best resource is yourself, using comfortably whatever simple materials and activities you and each individual child choose.

Whatever happens to children happens to and for their whole lives, and, through them, to their own children.

The children are everyone's heirs, everyone's business, everyone's future
(Piercy, 1987, p.183).

Bibliography

Adcock, M. with Dubois, D. and Small, A. (1988), 'Ending relationships successfully', in *Direct Work With Children*, J. Aldgate and J. Simmonds (eds.), pp.122–33, B. T. Batsford Ltd, London.

Adcock, M. with Lake, R. and Small, A. (1988), 'Assessing children's needs', in *Direct Work With Children*, J. Aldgate and J. Simmonds (eds.), pp.22–35, B. T. Batsford Ltd, London.

Ahmed, S., Cheetham, J. and Small, J. (eds.) (1986), *Social Work With Black Children and Their Families*, B. T. Batsford Ltd, London. In association with British Agencies for Adoption and Fostering.

Aldgate, J. (1988), 'Work with children experiencing separation and loss: a theoretical framework', in *Direct Work With Children*, J. Aldgate and J. Simmonds (eds.), pp.36–48, B. T. Batsford Ltd, London.

Aldgate, J. with Galley, J. (1988), 'Permanency planning for older children in care', in *Direct Work With Children*, J. Aldgate and J. Simmonds (eds.), pp.62–74, B. T. Batsford Ltd, London.

Aldgate, J. and Hawley, D. (1986), Helping foster families through disruption. *Adoption and Fostering*, 10 (2), pp.44–9, 58.

Aldgate, J. and Simmonds, J. (eds.) (1988), *Direct Work With Children: A Guide for Social Work Practitioners*, B. T. Batsford Ltd, London. In association with British Agencies for Adoption and Fostering.

Apley, J. (1980) in Wilkinson, S. (1987), 'Communication: making contact with children', in *Research Highlights in Social Work: 6*, J. Lishman (ed.), pp.53–72, Jessica Kingsley Publications, London.

Argent, H. (ed.) (1988, *Keeping The Doors Open: A Review of Post-Adoption Services*, British Agencies for Adoption and Fostering, London.

Ashley, B. (1974), *The Trouble with Donovan Croft*, Oxford University Press, London.

Asimov, I. (1988), *Prelude to Foundation*, Grafton (Collins), London.

Asrat-Girma (1986), 'Afro-Caribbean children in day care', in *Social Work With Black Children and Their Families*, S. Ahmed, J. Cheetham and J. Small (eds.), pp.40–50, B. T. Batsford Ltd, London.

Bacon, F. (1902: 1st ed. 1600), 'On truth', in *Essays*, Grant Richards, London.

Bainbridge, B. (1980), 'Grandma's central position', in *Dandelion Clocks*, A. Bradley and K. Jamieson (eds.), pp.60–5, Penguin, Harmondsworth.

Banks, E. and Mumford, S. (1988), 'Meeting the needs of workers', in *Direct Work With Children*, J. Aldgate and J. Simmonds (eds.), pp.101–110, B. T. Batsford Ltd, London.

Boseley, S. (1990), 'Embattled servants of the needy', *The Guardian*, 21 March, p.21.

Bradley, A. and Jamieson, K. (eds.) (1980), *Dandelion Clocks: Stories of Childhood*, Penguin, Harmondsworth.

Brandon, D. and Jordan, B. (eds.) (1979), *Creative Social Work*, Basil Blackwell, Oxford.

Brontë, C. (1966: 1st ed. 1847), *Jane Eyre*, Penguin, Harmondsworth.

Byars, B. (1977), *The Pinballs*, The Bodley Head, London.

Caird, G. B. (1963), *The Gospel According to St Luke: The Pelican New Testament Commentaries*, Penguin, Harmondsworth.

Campbell, B. (1988), *Unofficial Secrets: Child Sexual Abuse – The Cleveland Case*, Virago, London.

Carroll, L. (1865), *Alice's Adventures In Wonderland*. (1948: 1st ed. 1872), *Alice Through the Looking Glass*, Penguin, Harmondsworth.

Chamberlain, M. (1983), *Fenwomen: A Portrait of Women in an English Village*, Routledge & Kegan Paul, London.

Connor, T., Sclare, I., Dunbar, D. and Elliffe, J. (1984), 'A residential homefinding unit', *Adoption and Fostering*, 8 (4), pp.44–6, 72.

Crompton, M. (1980), *Respecting Children: Social Work with Young People*, Edward Arnold, London.

Crompton, M. (1982), *Adolescents and Social Workers*, Heinemann/Community Care, London.

Curtis, P. (1982), 'Communicating through play'. *Adoption and Fostering*, 6 (1), pp.27–30.

Dominelli, L. (1989), 'Betrayal of trust: a feminist analysis of power relationships in incest abuse and its relevance for social work practice.' *The British Journal of Social Work*, 19 (4), pp.291–307.

Dunbar, M. (1987), *Catherine: A Tragic Life – The Story of A Young Girl Who Died of Anorexia Nervosa*, Penguin, Harmondsworth.

Eliot, G. (1979: 1st ed. 1860), *The Mill On The Floss*, Penguin, Harmondsworth.

Ellis, D. J. (1981), 'Are we being educated?' (Presidential Address), in *New Vistas*, Guild of Friends in Education, London. Unpublished.

Erikson, E. (1965), *Childhood and Society*, Penguin, Harmondsworth.

Fisher, M., Marsh, P., Phillips, D. with Sainsbury, E. (1986) *In And Out of Care: The Experiences of Children, Parents, and Social Workers*, B. T. Batsford Ltd, London. In association with British Agencies for Adoption and Fostering.

Foreman, L. and A. (1985), Foster parents helping children to move. *Adoption and Fostering*, 9 (2), pp.54–5, 57.

Furman, E, (1974), *A Child's Parent Dies: Studies in Childhood Bereavement*, Yale University Press, New Haven and London.

Gardner, R. (1987), *Who says? Choice and Control in Care*, National Children's Bureau, London.

Goldacre, P. (1980), Helping children with bereavement, *Adoption and Fostering*, 4 (2), pp.37–40.

Grimm, J. and W. (trans Marshall, B.) *Fairy Tales*, Ward Lock & Co. Ltd., London.

Guild of Friends in Education (1981), *New Vistas: Report of Conference Held at Saffron Walden School*. Unpublished.

Halliday, J. (1990), 'The little children who suffer', *Hull Daily Mail*, 21 March, p.15.

Hapgood, M. (1988), 'Creative direct work with adolescents: the story of Craig Brooks', in *Direct Work With Children*, J. Aldgate and J. Simmonds (eds.) pp.87–100, B. T. Batsford Ltd, London.

Hill, S.   (1974),   *I'm The King of the Castle*, Penguin, Harmondsworth.
Holgate, E.   (1972),   Introduction, in *Communicating With Children*, E.
   Holgate (ed.), pp.xi-xv, Longman, London.
Hopkirk, E.   (1988),   'Introducing direct work with children to area teams
   in social services departments', in *Direct Work With Children*, J. Aldgate
   and J. Simmonds (eds.), pp.111–121, B. T. Batsford Ltd, London.
Hughes, R.   (1929),   *A High Wind in Jamaica*, Chatto & Windus, London.
Hunt, D.   (1982),   Preface, in *The World of Nigel Hunt: The Diary of a
   Mongoloid Youth*, N. Hunt, pp.13–26. Asset Recycling Ltd., Norwich
Hunter, M.   (1987),   'Julia: a frozen child'. *Adoption and Fostering*, 11 (3),
   pp.26–30.
Jansson, T.   (trans Warburton, T.: 1983),   'The Invisible Child', in *Tales
   from Moomin Valley*, pp.103–19, Penguin, Harmondsworth.
Jolly, J.   (1981),   *The Other Side of Paediatrics: A Guide to The Everyday
   Care of Sick Children*, Macmillan, Basingstoke.
Jones, M. and Niblett, R.   (1985),   'To split or not to split: the placement
   of siblings.' *Adoption and Fostering*, 9 (2), pp.26–9.
Korczak, J.   (1926–7),   The open window, in *Społeczeństwo*, 3, (1), quoted
   in Szlazakowa, A, trans., Ronowicz, E., 1978, *Janusz Korczak*,
   Wynawnictwa Szkolne i Pedagogiczne, Warsaw, p.42.
Korczak, J.   (1929)   *How to Love a Child, (Jak Kochać Dziecko)*, Warsaw,
   quoted in Szlązakowa, passim.
Korczak, J.   (1929)   *The Right of the Child to Respect*, Warsaw, quoted in
   Szlązakowa, p.138.
Krementz, J.   (1984),   *How It Feels to Be Adopted*, Gollancz, London.
Le Guin, U.   (1971),   *A Wizard of Earthsea*, Penguin, Harmondsworth.
Leonard, A.   (1988),   *Tinker's Career*, Walker, London.
Lishman, J. (ed.)   (1987),   *Research Highlights in Social Work, 6: Working
   with Children*, Jessica Kingsley Publications, London.
Little, J.   (1985),   *Mama's Going To Buy You a Mocking Bird*, Penguin,
   Harmondsworth.
Lurie, A.   (1989),   *The Truth About Lorin Jones*, Abacus (Sphere), London.
McCullers, C.   (1962),   *The Member of the Wedding*, Penguin,
   Harmondsworth.
MacDonald, G.   (1871),   *The Princess and the Goblin*, Blackie & Son,
   London, Glasgow, Dublin.
Madge, N. and Fassam, M.   (1982),   *Ask The Children: Experiences of
   Physical Disability in the School Years*, B. T. Batsford Ltd, London.
Magorian, M.   (1983),   *Good Night Mister Tom*, Penguin, Harmondsworth.
Marshall, J. (unpub), Gifts of the spirit.
Maximé, J. E.   (1986),   'Some psychological models of black self-concept',
   in *Social Work With Black Children and Their Families*, S. Ahmed, J.
   Cheetham, and J. Small (eds.) pp.100–116, B. T. Batsford Ltd, London.
Mennell, M.   (1986),   'The experience of Bradford Social Services
   Department', in *Social Work With Black Children and Their Families*, S.
   Ahmed, J. Cheetham, and J. Small (eds.), pp.120–131, B. T. Batsford Ltd,
   London.
Milne, A. A.   (1926),   *Winnie The Pooh*, Methuen, London.
Mitchell, D.   (1986),   'The mouse cage', in *Learners All*, Quaker Social
   Responsibility and Education, pp.7–8, Quaker Home Service, London.

Morgan, S. (1986), 'Practice in a community nursery for black children', in *Social Work With Black Children and Their Families*, S. Ahmed, J. Cheetham, and J. Small (eds.), pp.69–74, B. T. Batsford Ltd, London.

Morris, M. (1986), 'Communicating with adolescents'. *Adoption and Fostering*, 10 (4), pp.54–5, 71.

Müller, D. J., Harris, P. J., Wattley, L. A. (1986), *Nursing Children: Psychology, Research and Practice*, Harper & Row, London.

Norman, P. (1979), *The Skater's Waltz*, Hamish Hamilton, London.

Patterson, K. (1981), *The Great Gilly Hopkins*, Penguin, Harmondsworth.

Pearce, P. (1985), *The Way to Sattin Shore*, Penguin, Harmondsworth.

Piercy, M. (1987), *Woman On The Edge of Time*, The Women's Press Ltd., London.

Pierson, J. (1989), Book Review. *Social Work Education*, 8 (2), pp.41–2.

Quaker Social Responsibility and Education (1986), *Learners All: Quaker Experiences of Education*, Quaker Home Service, London.

Religious Society of Friends (1960, *Christian Faith and Practice in the Experience of The Religious Society of Friends*, London Yearly Meeting, London.

Reps, P. (compiler) (1971), *Zen Flesh, Zen Bones*, Penguin, Harmondsworth.

Rodin, J. (1983), *Will This Hurt?: Preparing Children for Hospital and Medical Procedures*, Royal College of Nursing of the UK, London.

Rose, E. (1988), 'Art therapy: a brief guide,' *Adoption and Fostering*, 12 (1), pp.48–50.

Rutter, M. (1983), *A Measure of Our Values*, Quaker Home Service, London.

Saint-Exupéry, A. de (trans. Woods, K.) (1974), *The Little Prince*, Pan, London.

Shaw-Champion, G. *Teaching Makaton to Chloe: A Family's Experience*, Down's Children's Association.

Smith, F. H. (1988), Book Review. *Social Work Education*, 8 (1), pp.44–6.

Stenbak, E. (1986), *Care of Children in Hospital: A Study*, World Health Organization, Copenhagen.

Striker (Hippo Books), *The Anti-Colouring Book*.

Szlązakowa, A. (trans Ronowicz, E.: 1978), *Janusz Korczak*, Wydawnictwa Szkolne i Pegagogiczne, Warsaw.

Taylor, E. (1986), *A Game of Hide and Seek*, Virago, London.

Taylor, E. (1967), *A Wreath of Roses*, Penguin, Harmondsworth.

Taylor, E. (1988), *At Mrs Lippincote's*, Virago, London.

Todd, R. J. N. (ed.) (1968), *Disturbed Children: Papers on Residential Work, 2*. Longman, London.

Torrie, A. (1978), *When Children Grieve*, Cruse, Richmond, Surrey.

Ure, J. (1987), *One Green Leaf*, The Bodley Head, London.

Walkerdine, V. and Lucey, H. (1989), *Democracy In The Kitchen: Regulating Mothers and Socialising Daughters*, Virago, London.

Watson, E. W. (1985), *The Art of Pencil Drawing*, Watson-Guptill Publishers, New York.

Webster, J. (1980), 'Rose would be a lovely name for it', in *Dandelion Clocks*, Bradley A. and Jamieson K. (eds.) pp.173–188, Penguin, Harmondsworth.

Weldon, F.   (1975),   *Female Friends*, Heinemann, London.

Wilkinson, S.   (1987),   'Communication: making contact with children', in *Research Highlights in Social Work, 6: Working with Children*, Lishman J.(ed.), pp.53–72, Jessica Kingsley Publications, London.

Wills, W. D.   (1971),   *Spare The Child: The Story of An Experimental Approved School*, Penguin, Harmondsworth.

Winnicott, C.   (1964),   'Communicating with children', in *Disturbed Children*, Todd R. (ed.), pp.65–80, Longman, London.

Wolkind, S.   (1988),   'Post-adoption work by the child psychiatrist', in *Keeping The Doors Open*, Argent H. (ed.) pp.100–101, British Agencies for Adoption and Fostering.

Author Index

Adcock, Margaret 29, 47, 76–7, 113
Aldgate, Jane 29, 31, 35, 36, 77, 104
Ashley, Bernard 93
Asimov, Isaac 10
Asrat-Girma 4, 106, 108, 111

Bacon, Francis 63
Bainbridge, Beryl 70–71, 104
Banks, Eva 5, 37, 41, 76, 109, 112
Boseley, Sarah 22
Brandon, David 77
Brontë, Charlotte 58, 68–9
Byars, Betsy 94

Caird, G. B. 82
Campbell, Beatrix 3–4, 41, 43, 87–9, 91, 100, 114
Carroll, Lewis 61, 68–9
Chamberlain, Mary 59
Connor, Terry 48
Crompton, Margaret v, 59–60, 71
Curtis, Patricia 74

Dominelli, Lena 8
Dubois, Dominic 29, 47, 76–7
Dunbar, David 48
Dunbar, Maureen 65

Eliot, George 33, 70, 87, 96–7
Elliffe, John 48
Ellis, D. June 72, 73, 74, 110
Erikson, Erik 54

Fassam, Meg 7, 104–5, 111
Fisher, Mike 29, 75
Foreman, Lily & Albert 48–9, 92, 100
Furman, Erna 35

Galley, Janet 77, 104
Gardner, Ruth 7, 105, 108
Goldacre, Patricia 27–8, 34, 37–8
Grimm, Jakob & Wilhelm 107

Halliday, Judith 40
Hapgood, Miles 74–5, 76, 77, 80, 83
Harris, Pam J. 36, 45, 59, 89, 90, 111, 114, 115

Hawley, David 29, 31, 35, 36
Hill, Susan 56–7, 57–8, 59
Holgate, Eileen 8
Hopkirk, Eve 91–2
Hughes, Richard 61
Hunt, Douglas 70
Hunt, Nigel 70
Hunter, Margaret 107

Jansson, Tove 105
Jolly, June 6, 7–8, 45, 46, 90–91, 95–6, 99–100
Jones, Mary 7

Korczak, Janusz 6, 116
Krementz, Jill 66

Lake, Roger 113
Le Guin, Ursula K. 56–7
Leonard, Alison 98
Little, Jean 38, 96, 97–8
Lucey, Helen 60–61
Luke, St. 81–3
Lurie, Alison 64–5

MacDonald, George 55
Madge, Nicola 7, 104–5, 111
Magorian, Michelle 107
Marsh, Peter 29, 75
Marshall, Josie 95
Maximé, Jocelyn Emama 32, 106
McCullers, Carson 60
Mennell, Mike 115
Milne, A. A. 97
Mitchell, Dennis 79–80
Morgan, Syble 106, 115
Morris, Mike 43
Muller, Dave J. 36, 45, 59, 89, 90, 111, 114, 115
Mumford, Sarah 5, 37, 41, 76, 109, 112

Niblett, Rosalind 7
Norman, Philip 66

Paterson, Katherine 99
Pearce, Philippa 78–9, 98, 109, 112
Phillips, David 29, 75

Piercy, Marge 3, 117
Pierson, John 34, 102

Reps, Paul 78
Rodin, Jocelyn 45–6
Rose, Elaine 4, 28–9
Rutter, Michael 80–81

Sainsbury, Eric 29, 75
Saint-Exupéry, Antoine de vi
Sclare, Irene 48
Shaw-Champion, Geoff 90
Small, Andrew 29, 47, 76–7, 113
Smith, Frances H. 4–5
Stenbak, Else 5–6, 33–4, 46, 114, 115
Striker 44
Szlązakowa, Alicja 6, 116

Taylor, Elizabeth 70, 91, 100, 110
Torrie, Alfred 28, 35, 37, 54, 89, 94–5, 102

Ure, Jean 92, 94

Walkerdine, Valerie 60–61
Watson, Ernest W. 77–8, 79
Wattley, Lesley A. 36, 45, 59, 89, 90, 111, 114, 115
Webster, Jan 71, 73, 74
Weldon, Fay 66–7
Wilkinson, Simon 8, 89
Wills, W. David 73
Winnicott, Clare 72
Wolkind, Stehen 89–90

Subject Index

Abortion 71
Abuse/assault 3, 8, 11, 12, 13, 20, 31, 34,
    40, 41, 42, 43, 47, 64, 73, 88, 89, 91,
    100, 102, 103, 105, 114
  incest 8, 66
  neglect 11, 66
  non-accidental injury (NAI) 16, 105
Access 16, 17, 18, 19, 20, 34, 47, 95, 102
Accident/injury 16, 21, 27, 30, 42, 43, 92,
    94, 95
  bruise 16, 30, 64, 92
  fracture 46
  scalded 96
Adolescent/teenager/young people v, 18,
    44, 54, 60, 71, 76, 80–1, 92, 96, 105,
    115
Adoption 3, 22, 27, 28, 36, 38, 65, 66, 77,
    104, 107
Afro-Caribbean 4, 106
Agencies, establishments, organizations
    Barnardo's 11
    Boundless Project 19, 111
    clinic 14, 40, 43, 45, 88
      child guidance 19–20, 70
    court (juvenile, magistrates') 11, 17, 18,
      20, 21, 30, 40, 44, 63, 65, 72, 102
    Cruse 28
    department of social security 11
    Dublin Sexual Assault Treatment
      Unit 43
    family centre 3, 9, 11–13, 41, 44, 102,
      113
      Ladywell Projet 11, 44, 113
      Rownberry House 12–13, 41, 44, 97,
      102
    Family Makers Homefinding Unit 48
      homefinding/team 4
    family placement unit i, 22, 44
    foster home see foster
    Friends of the Earth 53
    general practice 14
    hospice 15, 16
    hospital v, 5, 7, 10, 14–16, 22, 27, 28,
      29, 30, 34, 36, 37, 38, 41, 45, 46,
      59, 65, 71, 92, 94, 96, 97, 99, 104,
      105, 111, 114, 115

      ear nose and throat unit/ENT 46
      in-patient unit 80–81
      intensive care unit/ICU 16, 30, 46,
        95, 108
      mother and baby/maternity unit 14,
        91
      "Mummies' Ward" 65
      operating theatre 16, 46
      paediatric/ward/unit 3, 15, 30, 93,
        111, 114, 115
      plastic surgery department/ward 95
      psychiatric wing 14
      special care unit 28
    National Children's Homes/NCH 11,
      74
    National Society for the Prevention of
      Cruelty to Children/NSPCC 11, 40
    nursery 11, 21, 87, 92, 106, 108, 109,
      111
    prison 31, 104
    probation service/office 17, 18, 44, 112
    Religious Society of
      Friends/Quakers 67, 72
    school 11, 12, 20, 21, 27, 30, 32, 38, 41,
      69, 70, 89, 91, 93, 95, 103, 104, 111,
      115
      boarding 20, 72, 110
      experimental approved 73
      Sunday 54
      for backward children 70
    settlement, East End 68
    social services department/SSD v, 3, 21,
      22, 31, 88, 106
    The Children's Society 11
    voluntary agency/society 3, 14, 114
Anal dilation 88
Anger/angry 5, 13, 14, 20, 21, 22, 37, 42,
    46, 48, 71, 77, 79, 80, 81, 90, 91, 92,
    109
Anxiety/anxious 4, 16, 27, 31, 35, 38, 39,
    40, 41, 42, 43, 44, 45–6, 49, 55, 59,
    60, 61, 81, 87, 93, 94, 100, 109, 111,
    112–14
Asian 106, 108
Assess/ment 11, 12, 14, 19, 22, 28, 32, 40,
    43, 45, 49, 78, 113

Baby 6, 12, 13, 14–15, 16, 22, 28, 33, 59, 61, 68, 71, 90, 91, 92, 95, 96, 99, 100, 104, 107, 108
Bangladeshi 108
Black 4, 32, 93, 106, 111, 115
Brooke, Rupert 38

Care/er/ing v, 3, 4, 5, 7, 8, 17, 19, 23, 28, 29, 30, 31, 32, 34, 36, 38, 45, 47, 58, 59, 61, 65, 71, 74, 75, 78, 83, 88, 89, 91, 92, 93, 96, 103, 105, 106, 107, 109, 110–13, 114, 115, 116
  child 6, 13, 32, 106
  committal to 107
  day 4, 106
  discharge from/ending 29, 38
  entry/reception into 13, 29, 31, 32, 34, 38, 47, 107
  home on trial 21
  in 21, 22, 27, 30, 31, 32, 34, 37, 41, 47, 65, 92
  move within 29, 38, 47, 49
    and control 17
      order 21, 31, 63
    proceedings 20
  place of safety/order 30, 114
Children referred to more than once:
    pseudonyms, – not quoted in extracts
    from literature
  Cathy 20–21, 44
  Jim and Joe 4, 36
  Mandy 65, 72
  May 4, 42, 57, 59, 82, 91, 93, 97, 99, 110, 112
  Rosie 103, 108–9
  Roy 27, 33
  Sally 31, 33
Cleveland 3, 8, 87–8, 89, 114
Communication: methods and means of:
  animal/s 80, 92, 93–5, 96–8, 101, 115
    cat 18, 46, 94
      'Syrup' 112
    dog/puppy 3, 5, 21, 27, 43, 93, 94
      alsatian 27
      foster dog 31
      fox terrier 'Max' 94
      labrador 31
    guinea pig 93
    hamster 32
    mouse 79–80
    rabbit 93
      Superbun 93–4
    bird/s 35, 58, 101
      budgerigar 93, 94–5
      canary 97

    crow 57
    owl 'Hoot' 96
  fish 95
    'Fred' the goldfish 95
  insects 58
  pets 18, 30, 94
  body posture 18
  book/s v, vi, 4, 5, 6, 10, 23, 37, 55, 69, 96, 100, 111, 117
    Anti-Colouring 44
    comics 175
    exercise 15
    legend 103, 106
    life story 3, 4, 36, 48, 57, 91, 107–8
    magazines 99, 115
    myth 154
    novel 56, 57, 60, 64, 66, 92, 94, 98, 99, 100, 110, 111
    poetry 37–8, 69
    preparation for operation 46
      about me 13
    story/tale 5, 35, 38, 55, 70, 71, 78, 91, 93, 98, 100, 107, 111, 112
      fairy 59, 103
  candles 3, 29
  car journeys 30, 43
  cards 43
  cassettes/tapes 18, 48, 96
  clothes/clothing/dress 18, 33, 46, 48, 60, 61, 64, 70, 78, 87, 98, 103–6, 111, 116
  crying/weeping 5, 28, 32, 33, 36, 65, 79, 82, 89, 90, 91, 92, 93, 94, 101, 109
  cuddling 13, 15, 28, 36, 90, 91, 92, 93, 97, 101, 103
  doll 3, 5, 12, 16, 36, 37, 46, 47, 96–7, 102, 107, 111
    house 12, 74
    boy figures 74
  essay 37
  family tree 43, 99
  flow chart 75, 77
  food/drink/meals 19, 32, 36, 38, 42, 48, 71, 76, 82, 105, 106–110, 111, 112, 113, 115, 116
    cooking 11, 19
  fun/humour/laughter 8, 13, 16, 18, 40, 45, 47, 69, 71, 96, 97, 98, 107, 111
  games 40, 48, 58, 72, 75, 76, 78
    action 15
    arcade 74, 77
      The Pinballs 94
    backgammon 20
    finger 15
  gardening 102, 103
  letters 18, 44

Communications—*contd.*
  listening 3, 4, 5, 7–8, 12, 18, 23, 43, 44,
    66, 68, 72, 74, 75, 77, 79, 83, 90, 112,
    117
  looking/seeing *ii*, 3, 9, 10, 14, 18, 28, 41,
    43, 55, 57, 77–80, 83, 113
  magic 15, 40, 42, 45, 48, 61, 93, 103
    carpet 40
    ghost 58
    goblin 55
    magician 93
    monster 55–6
    seven leagued boots 70
    three wishes 17
    wizard 56
  Makaton 90
  mobiles 14
  music 19, 96, 101, 111, 15
    box 70
    dance 90
    sing 15, 69, 96
  painting/picture 14, 16, 17, 20, 32, 46,
    53, 55, 64, 91, 97, 98, 99, 100, 115
    /drawing 3, 5, 6, 43, 69, 78, 96, 117
    art therapy/work 4, 28, 29
    cutout work/figures 4, 21
    friezes 14
    murals 3, 16, 43
    pencils and paper 60, 102
    posters 16
  photocopy 13
  photograph/y 6, 16, 36, 74, 98, 101
  play/ing 5, 11, 12, 13, 14, 15, 41, 42, 46,
    69, 106, 111, 113, 114, 115, 116
    ground 103
    group 63, 64, 114
    room 3, 12, 13, 19, 20, 46, 47, 97,
      115
    cardboard people/paper houses 48
    clay/sand/water 3, 19, 20, 42, 106
  plays/drama 48, 78, 115
    role play 12, 13, 32
  silence 18, 38, 79, 87, 89, 116
  smile/ing 5, 15, 18, 19, 46, 89, 90, 91,
    101, 105
  sport/outdoor activities 43, 44
    caneoing/rafting 19
    climbing/mountaineering 19, 56–7
    cycling 19
    football 22, 44
    hiking/walking 19, 43, 74, 93
    potholing 19
    swimming 74
  talking/speaking 5, 7, 8, 12, 15, 16, 20,
    36, 41, 42, 44, 49, 71, 78, 83, 87–101,
    105, 112, 116

  telephone 13, 18, 21, 22, 66, 87, 112,
    114
  toy 13, 14, 15, 16, 17, 21, 43, 46, 96–8,
    101, 103, 104, 111, 115, 117
    cupboard 103, 115
    bean bags 13, 30
    car 17
    hair dryer 20
    lego 17
    puppet 48
      glove 12, 43, 97
    teddy 12–13, 96
      'Winnie-the-Pooh' 97
  video 46, 48, 77, 98, 100
  wait/ing 7, 23, 41, 42, 49, 56, 88, 101,
    107
  worksheets 13
Control 8, 13, 20, 31, 33, 55, 56, 58, 59,
  60, 61, 80, 100, 101, 104, 105, 109
  care and 17
  out of 32
Custody 17

Death/dead/die/dying 6, 7, 8, 15, 16, 20,
  23, 27, 28, 30, 33, 34, 35, 36, 37, 38,
  53, 54, 57, 58, 64, 65, 66, 72, 81, 83,
  91, 92, 94, 95, 96, 97, 98, 101, 104,
  107, 109
  bereaved 15, 16, 28, 35, 36, 37, 89
  burial/buried 15, 35, 38, 94, 104
  cemetery 38
  drown 42
  funeral 28, 37–8, 94, 104
  kill/ed 57, 69, 95, 107
  mortuary 28
  mourn/ing 33, 83
  suicide 37, 98
Despair/desperate 9, 10, 11, 33, 41, 70, 78,
  79, 80, 89, 109, 112, 113, 114
Divorce 19, 20, 34, 38

Education *v*, 6, 17, 27
Examination 30, 43, 49
  cross 63

Fear/fright 4, 5, 12, 16, 27, 32, 37, 41, 43,
  46, 49, 53–62, 65, 68, 72, 73, 76, 77,
  80, 82, 83, 87, 89, 91, 92, 93, 94, 111,
  117
Filipino 108
Foster/ing (child, home, parent) 3, 4, 5, 6,
  7, 10, 21, 22, 27, 28, 29, 31, 35, 36,
  42, 47, 48, 57, 67, 89, 91, 92, 93, 94,
  97, 99, 100, 104, 107–108, 109, 110,
  112, 114, 115
  boarded out 93, 105

Friend/ship 12, 27, 36, 37, 65, 66, 70, 92, 95, 103, 111

Grief 16, 27, 28, 32, 36, 38, 89, 91, 94, 100, 104
Guilt 22, 31, 34, 36, 39, 71, 82

Healer/healing 36, 42, 81, 82, 83, 94, 97
Honest/y *v*, 31, 44, 49, 60, 61, 65, 70, 76, 77, 80, 95, 117
Hope *vi*, 4, 6, 8, 10, 19, 57

Illness/disability
  AIDS 47
  anorexia nervosa 65
  arthritis 60, 92
  blind 73
  cancer 27, 53, 92, 96
  depression 27, 37, 41
    post-natal 14
  disabled 7, 14, 82, 87, 111
  Down's Syndrome 14, 70, 90
  handicap 16, 59, 60, 96, 102, 104
    mental 28, 90
  Hunchback of Notre Dame, The 59–60
  Huntington's Chorea 98
  illness/disease 16, 27, 28, 30, 37, 42, 47, 48, 53, 60, 72, 98, 101, 102, 113, 114
    terminal 15
  leukaemia 93
  mentally disturbed 87
  progressive degenerative disease 16
  spina bifida 104
  tonsils 45
  unconscious 16, 95, 101
  vaginal bleeding 41, 81–3

Jesus 81–3, 95

Law/legal *v*, 40, 63, 82, 116
Loss 7, 23, 27, 29, 30, 31, 32–4, 35, 36, 37, 38, 39, 42, 55, 83, 91, 94, 97
Love *v*, *vi*, 3, 4, 5, 6, 7, 8, 11, 14, 21, 23, 29, 31, 35, 36, 54, 63–7, 69–75, 81, 82, 87, 91, 92, 94, 96, 99, 101, 109, 110–111, 115, 116, 117

Mean/ing 5, 8, 67–75, 89, 96
Medical/medicine 4, 6, 14, 39, 45, 46, 49
  premedication 46

Offence/offenders/delinquent 18, 19, 44, 59, 80, 81, 96, 111
  crime/criminal 31, 79, 88
  sexual 31
  stealing/theft 70, 79, 89–90

Pain 4, 23, 33, 34, 35, 36, 37, 42, 45, 47, 48, 55, 58, 72, 77, 79, 80, 90, 91, 107
Peace/ful 32, 53, 79, 80, 82, 83
  prayer 54, 61
Philosophy *v*, 10, 49, 83, 108, 113, 117
Poland/Polish *v*, 6
Practitioners
  administrator/ion/ive *v*, 6, 10, 81
  adopter *see* adoption
  advocate 63
  anaesthetist 46
  apothecary 68
  artist/painter 64, 66, 77
  attendant (hospital) 46
  catering staff 108
  child care officer 32, 72
  child protection officer 40
  clergy 10
  divorce court welfare officer/CWO 3, 10, 17, 41, 43, 93, 112
  doctor *v*, 3, 7, 8, 10, 22, 37, 41, 45, 46, 60, 63, 88, 91, 105, 114
    consultant 27, 71
    general practitioner/GP 10, 19, 22, 28, 71
    paediatrician 8
  doctors mentioned other than authors of quoted texts
    Apley, J 8
    Buchanan, Michael 3
    Dr X 71
    Higgs, Marietta 88, 114
    Hobbs, Christopher 3
    Korczak, Janusz 6, 8, 116
    Woods, Moira 41, 43, 88, 91
    Wynne, Jane 3
  family centre workers 113
  family placement worker 74
  foster father/mother/parent *see* foster
  guardian ad litem/GAL *v*, 3, 4, 10, 20–21, 28, 30, 43, 44, 63, 64, 65, 72
  healer *see* healer
  health visitor/HV 3, 10, 11, 14–15, 40, 63, 96
  judge 10
  lecturer/lecturing *i*, 8
  magician 93
  magistrate 10, 18, 63
  management 114
  midwives 22
  nurse/nursing 3, 5, 6, 7, 15–16, 33, 36, 44, 45, 46, 89, 91, 94, 96, 100, 108, 111, 114, 115, 117
    community 10
    matron 65
    nursery 3, 10, 12, 14, 41, 106

nursery worker 111
paediatric 6, 10, 15–16, 90
school 10, 63
senior – manager 15
sister 15, 94, 95
student 16
police 3, 10, 88, 89, 102
detective 88
prince 10
princess 55
probation officer 17, 18, 40, 44, 96
professor 80–1
project leader 9, 11, 44, 113
psychiatrist/ry (child) 10, 19, 28, 71, 80–81, 89
psychologist 10, 61, 70
pupil 72, 73, 74, 78, 111
queen 107
secretary 18
social work/er *v*, 3, 4, 5, 6, 8, 10, 11, 19, 20, 21, 22, 28, 29, 30, 31, 32, 36, 40, 43, 44, 47, 48, 57, 63, 68, 71, 72, 74, 75, 76, 87, 89, 91, 92, 102, 106, 107, 113, 114, 117
child guidance 10, 102
keyworker 30, 44, 48, 108
residential 10, 41, 72, 74, 76, 78, 82, 105
housemother 87
Wilczynska, Stefania 6
assistant 4
senior officer 36
solicitor 10, 43, 65, 72
student *v*, 16, 21, 64, 68, 78
supervisor *see* supervision
teacher 10, 27, 28, 57, 63, 72, 78, 79, 91, 93, 110
head 70, 72, 73, 104
schoolmaster 87, 91
technician 6
therapist/therapy 5
art 4, 28–9
education 27
family 113
occupational 10
physio 10
psycho 107
speech 10
training officer *see* training
volunteer 79–80
Community Service 73
witness 63, 64
wizard 56
writer/writing 6, 8, 37
Practitioners referred to more than once:
pseudonyms,– not quoted in extracts
from literature

Barnes, Ellen 11, 44, 113
Bridge, Laura 17, 41, 43, 93, 112
Coombes, Sylvia 14, 40
Don, Pearl 4, 42, 57, 82, 83, 91, 93, 97, 99, 110, 112
Grant, Alec 18–19, 44, 96, 97
Harris, Ann 14–15, 96
Hill, Stella 20–21, 44
Hughes, Anna 15, 16, 30, 95
Kent, Elaine 12–13, 41–2, 44, 102
King, Helen 19–20, 102
Mint, Nancy 12, 13, 41, 42, 44, 102
Trent, Fran 21, 43
Wells, Kit 4, 5
West, Rachel 15–16, 28, 30, 36, 46, 91, 92–3, 94, 95, 97, 104, 105, 115

Religion *v*, 36, 108
Christian 6
Jewish 6, 66, 82
Muslim/Islamic 104, 108
Religious Society of Friends (Quakers) 67, 72
Residential 7, 21, 32, 72, 105, 106, 108, 110
adventures 19, 111
assessment centre 28
centre 29
community home 30, 31, 82
with education (CHE) 105
hostel 30
orphanage 6, 104
Korczak's Orphans' Home 6
remand/centre/home 18, 21, 29
residential/children's home 3, 20, 28, 31, 32, 41, 76, 104, 106, 108
retirement home 65
Respect/ing *v*, 6, 8, 14, 15, 42, 45, 59, 71, 106, 115, 117
Routine 34, 38, 39, 45, 47, 112

Social enquiry report/SER 18–19, 44
Spirit/ual *vi*, 49, 58, 69, 82, 83, 106
Step child/parent 20, 21, 47, 64, 88, 103, 107, 109
Supervision/supervise/supervisor 17, 31, 36, 37, 68, 76, 105, 112, 114
order/SO 5, 18–19, 21, 30, 32
Support *v*, 8, 14, 15, 16, 19, 23, 27, 36, 37, 48, 81, 113, 114, 117
Surgery 5, 31, 49, 94, 115, 117
cardiac 46, 47, 94
operation 16, 37, 47
adenoids 65
amputation 31, 94
tonsils 45
tracheotomy 95

Training/officer 3, 4, 8, 12, 19, 23, 34, 48, 56, 78, 82, 104, 106, 117

Treblinka 6

Trust 8, 11, 13, 42, 46, 53–62, 65, 67, 93, 94, 102, 110, 111, 114, 116

Truth 5, 7, 8, 13, 14, 34, 35, 37, 39, 45, 47, 55, 61, 62, 63–7, 68, 69, 75, 89, 98, 103, 117
  un- 35, 46

lie/lying 11, 35, 64, 65, 67

Upanishads 53, 61

West Indian 106

White 32, 108, 111, 115
  Snow 107

Zen 77, 78